9/15

00658431

THE PLAIN CHOICE

A TRUE STORY OF CHOOSING
TO LIVE AN AMISH LIFE

SHERRY GORE

WITH JEFF HOAGLAND

ZONDERVAN

The Plain Choice
Copyright © 2015 by Sherry Gore

This title is also available as a Zondervan ebook. Visit www.zondervan.com/ebooks.

Requests for information should be addressed to:
Zondervan, 3900 Sparks Dr. SE, Grand Rapids, Michigan 49546

ISBN: 978-0-310-33558-0

The author is represented by The Steve Laube Agency, LLC.

Cover design: James Hall
Cover photography: Barbara Banks Photography
Interior design: Kait Lamphere

First printing June 2015 / Printed in the United States of America

This book is dedicated to
Jacinda, Shannon, and Tyler—
I am so grateful to be your mother

And to Denise—
you're still my best friend after all these years

CONTENTS

Prologue

THE GIRL ON THE CURB

"You don't know anything about me."

From all outward appearances, this could have been true. She was a young African American girl, her face ash gray and swollen, cratered like the moon. She'd been hit. More than once. I, on the other hand, was pink with summer sunburn, in a pastel dress and a white head covering.

I belonged to the Plain community. She, I was nearly certain, made her living as a prostitute.

What could we possibly have in common? More than she might think.

I was standing outside Sarasota Memorial Hospital when I first saw her. My daughter, Jacinda, was in day treatment for a six-hour infusion, and I'd stepped outside to find someplace to have lunch. The young girl was slumped against a hospital bench, an ID band from the ER around her wrist, the wounds on her cheek fresh.

She looked so frail she could've floated down from the sky and gotten stuck on the fresh paint of the bench.

"Hello?" I said, walking up to her. "Are you waiting on someone?"

She shook her head. Her lips were crusted white and chapped.

"Ma'am?" the hospital valet said. "Your van's ready."

I stepped closer to the girl. "Look, can I give you a ride somewhere?"

"Where?"

Her response told me so much. People only say "where" when there's no place to go.

"Your choice," I said.

She rubbed her nose on her sleeve. "Sure. Okay."

I had to help her into my van, and I brushed close to her bruised face while buckling her seat belt. It broke my heart. Hers was a face without hope. I knew that face. I'd worn it myself.

"I can understand why you live like you do," I said, climbing into the driver's seat. I wanted to reach out to her, make her less afraid. But she was hardened by her life.

"You don't know anything about me."

"Maybe not the details, no. But I can imagine you've made some tough choices. I've made a few tough choices too."

She glanced at my Plain dress. "You're nothing like me."

I shifted in my seat to face her directly. Curled against the door, she looked just like my daughter had looked during long trips to a Cincinnati hospital, in the early days.

"Listen ... I don't have any answers for you," I said. "I don't have any idea what you've faced in your life, what you've done, or what's been done to you. But I want you to know something." I caught her eyes with mine. "I want you to know that I care for you."

"What?"

"You heard me. I care for you."

"Gimme a break," she said.

"Listen to me." I touched her shoulder. "I care. Do you hear that? Listen to my words. I *care*. And I'm not alone." I pointed upward. "God. Him too. He loves you."

It was all I knew to say in that moment—a simple declaration of the only real truth I know in this world. I care. He loves. That's all. And happily, the warmth of those words broke her resolve a bit, and I saw the face of a scared little girl bubble up from the darkness below.

"We're closer than you think," I said to her. "Don't confuse what I wear with who I am. This dress doesn't say I'm perfect. It says that I am not."

Quiet tears licked at her face. "I ... I just can't get anything right."

"I couldn't either."

"I'm so ashamed ..."

"I was too."

She fell into her hands, then told me about her boys, ages six and seven, who lived with their grandmother since they didn't have a house of their own. She said she took "street jobs" to save up for an apartment.

"But it don't even matter," she continued, "because my boys will grow up, and they'll learn what I do, and they'll never understand. They'll hate me for what I've done."

"They won't," I said.

"It's true—I know it."

"Okay, so make them proud of you instead. Do what I did. Find the love in your heart and let it guide you."

She blinked slowly. "Love ... that's the one thing I can't ever seem to find."

I smiled and patted her hand. Then I took a deep breath, and I told her right then and there how it was that I found love; I told her my story, one heart to another in a van parked outside of a hospital. And when I was finished with the telling, and we finished crying, I drove her to a corner street in nearby Bradenton, where she said she "knew some people."

When she stepped down onto the sidewalk I knew I'd never

see her again. But I prayed as she walked away that she would find her own love, just like I did—even if, like me, she found it in the most unexpected of places.

Orange County, California, is a home for the fabulously rich, the famous, and the fortunate, where Botox and detox clinics live on the same block, and bleach blondes practically grow on trees. It's home to Newport Beach, Disneyland, and Surf City USA—and at one time, it was home to me.

Of course, I was a bleach blonde then, just like the rest. I spent my days racing a motorcycle around LA and my nights on-mic as a disc jockey.

My days look quite different now.

My name is Sherry Gore, and I am an Amish-Mennonite woman.

It's natural to wonder how I got from one lifestyle to the other—spray tan to a head covering. The journey was quite a ride, taking me across the country and back again, and there were times in between when I didn't know if I would make it out the other side. It's a complicated tale, but one worth telling because of a simple truth at its center:

I made a choice. A plain choice.

We all make hundreds of minor choices every day, but some can change the course of a life. Some choices define who we are or set into motion events too unimaginable to foresee and too overwhelming to understand.

My choice did both.

Today my home is Pinecraft, Florida, a sun-kissed Amish community nestled in Sarasota about five miles from the beach, and about five feet from some of the finest Amish cuisine in the world. Most days you'll spot me pedaling through my snowbird community on a Hawaiian-motif, cream-colored Electra bicycle with an eye-catching wicker basket. I'm the one in a blue dress with a white head covering, probably on Kaufman Avenue next to Big Olaf Ice Cream or riding down Beneva with some fresh produce from Yoder's Fresh Market. It's my own Amish version of the Sunset Strip, and it couldn't be farther from my days riding down beaches in a bikini with my curly blond hair blowing in the breeze.

I rent an efficient three-bedroom bungalow I share with my son, Tyler, my daughter, Jacinda, and my hound dog, Roxie. Tyler likes to fish, and Jacinda loves horses, but she is forced to love them from afar on account of her debilitating chronic illness.

Shannon, my middle child, used to live with us, but she married a dashing young man who swept her off her feet and all the way up to Canada, where they live an idyllic ranching life in a Mennonite community.

We have no television in my house, but as my writing career has grown, I've had to bring laptops, iPads, and the internet into our home. I'm thankful that my Amish and Mennonite friends in Pinecraft, some of whom spent years without electricity, have supported my efforts. Formerly, I published a national cooking magazine, *Cooking & Such*—it wasn't something one could put out in longhand.

So yes, I have electricity and I use some technology—but that doesn't mean I'm not Plain or not a part of the Plain community. There are other Amish and Mennonite communities throughout America where driving a car or owning a cell phone or turning on an electric light is as common as it is in New York City (though we traditionally have less traffic). Pinecraft is one of those places—every home is wired for electricity—and while most days I prefer to be on my bicycle, my minivan is always parked out front, just in case.

So what makes a Plain community then? Well, in short, *Plain* means Anabaptist—a branch of Protestant Christianity that favors strong community, simple living, and a focus on God above all else. We look to the Bible and to God for our moorings. *Plain* does not mean drab or colorless or boring; in fact, Amish and Mennonite culture sparkles with an eccentricity that has fascinated people across the globe. Ours is a beautiful and complex subset of contemporary American life, and I'm proud to be a part of a culture whose resilience is only matched by its capacity for love, for forgiveness, and for grace.

Sometimes, when I wake early in the morning to take Roxie for a walk, and I look down the row of simple Amish houses hugging mine, I just can't believe all that's happened in my life. I can't believe I finally found a place where I belonged. I'm very grateful.

But it took a long, long time.

You see, I made more mistakes than most. At times, I put myself so far away from where I needed to be that I couldn't see my way out. I kept starting over, each time hitting a Reset button with nothing to show for my effort. But I kept at it. And that's my advice to anyone who is struggling.

Keep at it.

It's what I said to the young girl at the hospital. I've known feelings of worthlessness. I've been judged. She looked at my head covering and my simple dress, and she thought, "You could never understand me."

But I do understand. I was crippled and I was blind. And I realize that I didn't find God in spite of my failings.

I found Him because of them.

Chapter 1

APRIL

It was almost Christmas.

My little sister April called in the evening, but I wasn't home; I was in the park with my friend Fannie watching Amish men play shuffleboard. Snowbird season was at its height in Pinecraft, when busloads of Amish and Mennonite people head south to ring in the New Year with laughter, old friends, and a healthy dose of ice cream.

Plump smiling women clogged Kaufman Avenue, trading status updates with friends just emerged from harvest, while men leaned against their bicycles to swap stories of corn silage and thresher mishaps.

At Pinecraft Park, young girls blushed at boys from across volleyball nets, hearts and minds inflamed, while bearded men resembling garden gnomes pet pink-leashed wiener dogs carping at squirrels.

Even English (non-Amish) folks strolled through, forever wishing to understand these mystifying people who earn simple lives with hard labor and ratify their choice in faith.

It was a far cry from where I grew up in Orange County; there wasn't a drop of spray tan or hubris to be found.

And while my sister April and I had bonded as California girls, ours was a love that could cross any line, including a cultural one. I supported her through her struggles with addiction even as I entered the Plain community. I shared my love for Jesus. I knew she would likely never follow my Plain path, but we stayed close in geography and in spirit, and it was a rare day when she didn't enter my thoughts.

But thinking of a person and hearing them are two different things. And as I walked through Pinecraft Park with Fannie on that wonderful December evening, I had no idea my sister was desperately trying to reach me on my home phone. I wish I had, because maybe I could've stopped what was soon to come. Maybe I could've heard her and things would've been different. But she was in her world and I in mine.

And sometimes that's just too far away to reach.

At six o'clock the next morning the phone rang again, and this time I was home to pick it up. The caller ID said "April." It wasn't like her to call so early.

"Hey, April, what's wrong?"

She didn't answer. I heard panting on the other end of the line, as if someone were running.

"April?"

A crash, something large shattering over the floor, and then muffled sobs.

"Hello?"

Footsteps and a grunt, then a high-pitched yell and Joe, April's boyfriend, screaming into the phone: "She won't wake up!"

"What?"

"April! Oh God, she's blue and the ambulance is here!"

"Wait ... no, what do you mean? Joe, what's happening?"

"April's dead! She's dead! 911's here and they said she's dead!"

"Oh God ..."

His voice crackled over the line, "She's blue! She's blue!"

The line went dead.

I fell against the refrigerator and pressed my face into the cold door.

"... April."

Then I was moving to the bedroom. Open the door. Wake up Shannon.

"What?" she asked in the dark.

"Something's happened; get on your clothes and wake up Tyler."

"What's happened?"

"Get on your clothes and wake up Tyler."

Get to the other room. Wake up Jacinda.

"Jacie," I whispered, rubbing her arm. "Jacie, wake up."

She'd been in bed for months. I didn't know what to tell her.

"What, Mom?"

"Listen . . ." Her face small and pale in the half-light. "I think something's happened to April, and we have to go."

"What happened?"

"I think she might be gone."

"What? What do you mean *gone*?"

Tyler, my fourteen-year-old, stepped into the room. "Mom what is it?"

Shannon appeared behind him. I looked from them to Jacinda and back.

"April's dead," I said, "and we have to go right now."

I put my hand on Jacinda's cheek. In her condition, she could not manage the trip, and I knew I would need all my energy in the next hour. I would have to leave her behind.

"I'm sorry," I told her. As I closed the door to her bedroom, an angling shaft of light caught the bottom of her shaking mouth.

Shannon had a cell phone, and so she called her boyfriend, Richard, who was visiting from Canada, to drive us the six miles to April's apartment. I was in no state of mind to drive.

The three of us—Shannon, Tyler, and I—crept out of my quaint ranch-style house, with its motto on the kitchen wall, like many Mennonite houses have, and into the darkness outside, where Richard would soon ferry us to the low-rent and seedy apartment complex April called home.

It was like I was about to travel back in time—from a world I'd chosen, to the one I'd barely escaped.

Richard arrived quickly and we loaded into his van. The roads were clear, and the traffic lights stayed green all the way, though when I looked at them, I saw nothing but the bloodiest red.

When we turned onto my sister's street, the front windshield lit up with blue flashing lights, and my sister's apartment—a place I'd been to many times—was covered in a labyrinth of bright yellow caution tape. A man in the parking lot took photographs. Three or four deputies circled a woman wearing a black business suit. Tyler counted fourteen emergency vehicles in all. The scene looked fake, like a crime movie set waiting for the stars to arrive.

Richard parked the van in front of April's apartment building, and as I approached the deputy, he must've recognized something in my face he'd seen before, because he knew immediately, in spite of my head covering, what I was there to do. I didn't waste any words.

"Is it true?" I asked. "Is she dead?"

He frowned. "Yes. I'm afraid she's gone."

My little sister April, who as a child had giggled into her hand when I first showed her a newborn Jacinda and told her, "April, you're an auntie now," was *gone*. The grief was unexplainable. My body numbed.

"Where is she?" I managed.

"Inside, on the couch."

His words were so frank, as if April were just inside, waiting patiently for me to take her from this place. To protect her like I'd always promised. But I couldn't protect her here, in this world I had left. And now she was gone.

Someone handed me a thick manila envelope, and I turned

to find a woman in a black suit standing close. "It's a victim's assistance crime package," she said. "You will look at it later on, and you might not remember much about what's happening right now." She put her hand on my shoulder. "But you need to remember you can call this number written on the top. The detective will answer your questions. Can you remember that?"

"Yes."

"What will you remember?"

"Call you."

"Yes." She sighed and looked to the apartment. "I'm so sorry it ends like this. We're familiar with April and Joe."

"You are?"

"We've been here before. She would call 911 and have him arrested for battery or child abuse, and we'd take him downtown. But then she'd show up the next morning and bail him out."

"I didn't know."

She shook her head. "People rarely do."

"Listen," she continued, "I want you to know that every time we came over here the boys were clean and fed. Every time. We don't always see that. She loved those boys."

I could barely whisper. "Where are they now?"

"Sequestered in the back bedroom with Social Services. We're about to bring them out."

"Do they know what has happened?"

"Not yet. As their next of kin, you'll have to tell them."

The sheriff's deputy then described what was happening inside the apartment, and I was left to imagine the rest: police officers form a human wall, shoulder to shoulder, across April's dingy apartment, flashing blue lights streaming in through dusty blinds. A woman smiles and takes the hands of two boys, ages six and eight, and leads them out of a darkened bedroom, down a short hallway, and past the shielded body of their dead mother. Neither boy knows to look. Neither will ever forget.

From the sidewalk, I saw my nephews emerge carrying their favorite stuffed animals. The boys were so small the deputy had to kneel on the ground to speak to them, and when he pointed at me they waved—two little cherubs blinking into police lights.

"Come here," I called to them.

They bounced from the steps wearing superhero backpacks. I wished I could make their short walk down the sidewalk last an eternity because I knew that when they got to me, and I folded them into my arms, their lives would never be the same again.

Before they could reach me, however, the silence halted short.

"They are *not* allowed to go with her!"

Joe had emerged from the far side of the parking lot. He was screaming into the early morning hour.

"This isn't right! They're staying with me! I'm their fath—"

"No," I said, surprising even myself at the granite surety of my voice. "You will shut your mouth right now."

He stopped, looked to the police.

"Don't look at them; they won't help you," I said. "I'm taking these children home."

I could tell he was wavering. Finally, he stepped back.

I motioned for the boys. "Come now, you two. Get in the van."

They took my hand and hopped into the vehicle as Joe slunk back into the night. Then Richard drove us away from those awful blue flashing lights.

At home an hour later, in my plain living room on Ponder Street, I told my two nephews their mother was dead. They didn't cry or ask questions. They fondled their toys and muttered "okay" or "you already said that." Their little brains just couldn't process it. So I told them everything and I told it straight. Then when I was finished, we had ice cream and ran through the house playing hide-and-seek, like nothing had happened at all.

The autopsy was completed by noon that same day. When

the medical examiner called, I stepped outside the house so I could be alone as he took me through the results. It was a horrifying conversation. April's heart had been in bad shape.

I was still on the phone with the examiner when Shannon walked outside and motioned for me to come into the house. I cupped my hand over the receiver.

"What is it?"

"It's Aunt Somara. She's on the other line. "

"Okay. Tell her I'll call her right back."

"Mom, hang up, it's important."

"I'm talking with the medical examiner."

She went back inside, but then a minute later came right back out again. "Mom," she said firmly, "I think you should hang up the phone and talk to Aunt Somara."

"Really?"

She nodded.

I started to tell the examiner I had to go, but he interrupted me instead.

"Listen Sherry," he said quickly, "I have an urgent call on the other line that I must take. I'll have to call you later, okay?"

"Yes."

I hung up and walked into the house. Shannon was still on the other line with my sister. She looked up at me from the couch.

"Joe's gone," she said.

"He skipped town?"

"No, Mom. He's dead."

"What do you mean?"

Somara had told Shannon that Joe killed himself. Joe's brother, who told Somara, said it was because Joe was afraid of being arrested for April's death. I then realized why the medical examiner had hung up so quickly: there was another body for him to examine.

Ultimately April's death was ruled an accidental overdose, even though her boys had seen Joe slip pills into her drink the night she died. I guess there's no homicide if there's no murderer alive to arrest. April was cremated and put in a vase with dolphins on the side. She loved dolphins.

But dolphins attract sharks, the kind who don't quit eating until the food is gone. And Joe was that kind of animal. He used my sister. She cashed in her stocks and bonds for him; he gambled her tax returns away; he spent her savings until her car was repossessed. And when he was finished—when all the food was gone—there was nothing left of her but a crumbled body lying on a couch.

I have no words to describe the funeral afterward. I remember little of it, save the friends and family who shared the burden of my grief, and one specific realization I had when it was over.

That realization was this: for most of my life I had been April. Our paths were identical. New beginnings, new mistakes, self-destructive behavior, depression, violence, rock bottom, and new beginnings again—an endless cycle of failure and regret.

But in the middle of my life something happened, something that pushed me out of the living nightmare I shared with my sister, and into something else. Otherwise it might've been Sherry Gore placed under soft light in a funeral home.

April died. I was saved. I do not know why God chose for it to be that way. But the least I can do is to tell my story. And remember my sister in the telling.

Chapter 2

THE OC

Carl Harris stood a shade under six feet, and his family called him Butch; he was one of those guys who got a perfect nickname early in life. His jokes, his stories, his reddish beard, and his strawberry blond hair made him a gravitational force at social gatherings. When Carl met someone for the first time, he or she wasn't likely to forget the moment.

My mom was no exception.

They were very young when they met. A quiet and reserved girl, she walked into her parents' living room one afternoon and found Carl sitting on the couch. He told her he'd seen her standing next to a tree the day before and had become so distracted he almost lost control of his car. He'd already decided they should be married. Things like that happened back then.

They were husband and wife not long after. She was seventeen. He was twenty-one.

The wedding was a union of disparate families. Mom came from down-South Georgia Southern Baptist Masons, with an ancestral line traveling back to eighteenth-century Lutherans in Alsace, France, while Dad's father was a judge at Derby Lane Greyhound Racing and founder of the Lealman Fire Department in St. Petersburg, Florida.

But bride and groom had one thing very much in common— they both wished to escape the lives already planned out for them.

After the wedding they moved to Dallas, which was bubbling

over with new industry on account of a futuristic technology few people understood—computing. It was 1965, and computers were the size of a shotgun house, difficult to access, and even harder to understand. But Dad, a mathematics whiz who could multiply four-digit numbers in his head, perceived them as the future and went to Dallas to get an education.

He threw himself into the study of computers, working a menial job during the day and pouring over programming books at night. While other young couples were out dancing or catching Hitchcock's latest thriller at the drive-in theater, Dad stayed home, taught himself to code, and planned for a career certain to defy expectations.

His work paid off quickly, and by the mid-1960s, when I was born, Dad was already head of the computing department at Imperial Van Lines moving company. He bought the house we lived in for $5,000 cash, and my first memory is throwing up on its multicolored terrazzo floor. I couldn't have been more than two years old.

My second oldest memory is from the day they introduced me to Wayne, my younger brother. Mom brought him into the house wrapped in a yellow blanket, and his head was as pink as an embarrassed flamingo. I thought he was an ice cream cone and introduced myself with a lick.

Wayne and I were born into the roaring 1970s: women's lib and the Vietnam War and *The Sonny and Cher Comedy Hour*. I don't remember my parents ever fighting, and Dad's infectious personality made our house a popular venue for cool people looking to smoke cigarettes, drink beer, and talk politics. They threw all sorts of parties, and their friends grooved on the type of house where Johnny Cash blared through the speakers while Wayne and I made blanket forts under the kitchen table.

That's how it was in the Harris household—easy breezy. Which is why I was so confused when my mom came into my room late at night, about three years after Wayne was born, to tell me that she and my father were getting a divorce. She was crying, and I'll never forget how helpless I felt. I had barely begun to enter the world, and just when I got there I found it was already broken.

Why did she want a divorce? I never did learn from her directly. I think maybe she needed something else, something we couldn't provide her. Regardless, Dad moved out of the house soon after. He was crushed.

Wayne and I stayed with our mom, and for a time it seemed we'd found a new normal. But then one afternoon a white van pulled to the front of our house, and two men went inside. They came back out again carrying my brother's clothes and toys in cardboard boxes.

The next morning, Wayne was on a plane to California— Orange County, to be specific, an odd place where everything is about class: low class, no class, high class. Money and status are equal tender, and people spend both liberally. Silicon Valley was ascendant then, and Southern California offered someone with Dad's abilities an enormous amount of opportunity. In Texas, he could be successful; in Orange County, he could be rich.

Dad didn't move there alone; a few months after the divorce, he married a beautiful woman named Chris who turned heads wherever she went. She wore white lip gloss and had long black hair like a Native American princess. Wayne and I liked her from the start.

My brother lived in California almost four years before I decided to join him, a difficult choice for any ten-year-old to make, but one I never regretted. After Dad left, I sensed something missing in my mother, some integral ingredient that must exist for a mother-daughter relationship to flourish. And I missed having a family.

Mom allowed me to fly out to Orange County to see if I

liked it there, and then, two months later, right before I was to start fifth grade, she flew out herself.

We were in a motel when I told her what I wanted to do.

"Dad said I could stay if you let me," I said.

"What do you want to do?" she asked.

"Stay."

She flew back to Florida alone.

In 1976, California was in the thick of the second skate-boarding boom, and I found Dad's community, Garden Grove, awash with young boys racing down sidewalks, teenage girls hula-hooping in driveways, and young children flailing desperately on skates.

The first friend I made was Denise, and we bonded simply, as children do, over a shared birthday. We were best friends less than an hour later—skating after school, playing hide-and-seek with boys at dusk, and playing with Barbies deep into the night.

That first year I enjoyed my new life in California. I rarely got into trouble, and I enjoyed the full attention of my dad and Chris—who took to me like a second mother. But in sixth grade everything changed when Chris learned she was pregnant with her first daughter, Somara. April followed two years later.

After my half-sisters were born, the new pecking order was apparent: Chris *liked* Wayne and me, but she *loved* Somara and April. The tremendous gulf between those two verbs—*like* and *love*—was clear the moment Chris brought her girls home, when suddenly it was as if Wayne and I were erased from her memory. Even worse, it was as if we were erased from Dad's memory too.

It felt like there were now two families living in our home: Chris's family and Carl's kids. Dad never missed one of April's or Somara's dance recitals, but when I had a softball game, or when Wayne had a Cub Scout meeting, even on a Saturday when my dad didn't work, Dad said he was busy. I became accustomed to my friends' parents cheering me on during sporting events.

It was as if Dad suddenly became a different man, a caretaker instead of the loving father I'd known before. And when it was time for family photos, we did two sets. One set featured April and Somara, and it went out to Chris's and Dad's families. The other set, with Wayne and me, went out to our mom.

By the time I entered junior high school, I was so sick of being ignored in my own home that I'd already figured out, as many children do, that it felt better to be punished than to be forgotten. So in service of being *seen*, I began to seek trouble wherever I could.

Denise and I were still best friends, and we shrugged off homework to do things like going on an awkward first date with two boys, sipping orange soda, and blushing on the patio of Burrito Bravo. Or in the summer we'd take the city bus to the beach and boogie-board until dark. We spent whole weekends at the mall.

I rarely turned in assignments or studied for tests, and so, of course, my grades fell year after year. And then when Denise moved away during eighth grade, my grades plummeted even further.

The worst of it came the day I brought home a report card with all F's—even in math, Dad's favorite subject. He was furious. He'd built his life on hard work and brains, and he took my poor grades as a personal rebuke.

"Don't you grow up to be some flunkie," he said, crinkling my report card in his hands. "I just won't have it."

"I'm trying, Dad, but in math the numbers don't make sense to me."

"You're not trying—you're lazy. I know you're not stupid because I'm not stupid. Math is easy if you just try. But you won't. Because you don't care enough. And do you know what we call people who don't care enough?"

"What?"

"Flunkies, Sherry. Flunkies."

That word was anathema to him, and when he uttered it his mouth curled up tight under his nose, as if his lips refused to take part in what he was saying. But I forced him to say it a lot, both because I was frequently in trouble, and because it was all he ever had to say to me when I was. There were no heartfelt confessionals. There were no supportive "hang in there, kid"–type expressions. He was stoic and sincere, like the Old Order Amishmen I'd meet years later, in a different life—but without their sense of forgiveness or warmth.

I only made it through junior high because my counselor thought it a shame to hold me back. She knew I read voraciously and that I was capable when I applied myself. Plus, as a counselor, she probably figured the stigma of being held back might do more damage to my life than having crummy algebra skills.

So I moved on to Los Alamitos High School, the kind of place where the principal drove a Porsche and the self-obsessed cliques could've appeared in a John Hughes movie: there were the "Dinosaurs," who wore rock shirts and smoked cigarettes behind the gymnasium with the "Punks" and the "Rockabillies"; the cheer team, who only dated the "Preps" and the "Richies;" and the "Jocks"—aqua-jocks, football meatheads—who pretty much ran the entire school.

I didn't belong to any of those cliques. I mostly stayed to myself and skipped math class whenever I could. Of course truants never escape punishment for long, and when my math teacher realized I was skipping, she leveled me with six weeks of Saturday school. It really wasn't "school" at all: we were given trash bags, gloves, and brooms, and "instructed" to clean the school grounds top to bottom.

On the first Saturday I had to report, I could hardly keep my eyes open, for I'd stayed up all night finishing *Flowers in the Attic* by V. C. Andrews. Unfortunately for me, Mr. Gibson, our hulking football coach and Saturday school chaperone, noticed my red eyes the moment I hit the door and came to a quick conclusion—Sherry Harris has been smoking "the reefer."

"If you ever come here loaded again, I'll have your butt expelled permanently!" he screamed. "And don't think because you're a girl I won't. You hear?"

"Of course I hear you."

"What do you mean *of course*?"

"Well—" I couldn't help myself—"you *are* yelling it right into my face."

That little bit of sass sent him right into orbit, and twenty minutes later my father received a phone call.

"Your daughter Sherry is a weed-smoking, talky, good-for-nothing who is one step away from getting kicked out of this school," Mr. Gibson said.

Which is how I found myself in the living room, listening to my father tell me how truly, truly disappointed he was by my behavior. And apparently, something else.

"You look just like her with your hair cut that way."

"Who?"

"Your mother."

It wasn't surprising to hear that when my father looked at me he saw someone else, that he saw my mother. I was right in front of him and he couldn't see me at all. Didn't know me at all.

And when a father doesn't know his own daughter, it's real hard for that daughter to know herself.

Chapter 3

GIRL POWER

I was a stranger in my own home. My father saw in me his greatest heartbreak. Chris had her "own family" to raise. And Wayne grew distant, foreshadowing the troubled, solitary man he would become.

Our house was an emotional vacuum; often I would sit up in my room, enjoying all the space in the world and yet gasping for air.

When my first troubled year at Los Alamitos High ended, Dad had no idea what to do with me, and I felt like I was breaking apart. I needed something else, something fresh. April and Somara were engaged and active in events all over town, and everywhere I turned I was in someone's way. We all needed a break. I needed a release.

It finally came with a change of scenery.

My aunt Judy and uncle Bill lived ninety miles south of Orange County on a five-acre mini-ranch in Escondido. Dad thought it a good idea to send me down there for the summer. Escondido was rural and quaint, and I think he hoped some simple farm living might do me good. So when Aunty Judy sent word back that I was welcome in her home, I caught a train south for the hinterlands.

What I found in Escondido was relief. Away from the rigors of ultrarich Orange County, I was able to spread my wings and learn a little responsibility. I helped Judy and Bill with chores around the farm and enjoyed home-cooked meals with them at night. I even met a handsome country boy. On weekends, he and I would ride a 1981 Honda CT70 trail bike out to Jake's Lake, where the anise plants made the air smell like licorice, and spend afternoons walking trails or watching local boys shoot frogs with .22 rifles.

It did wonders for my self-confidence. Aunt Judy and Uncle Bill encouraged me to be myself, and the people in their community seemed to like who I was. It felt light-years from Los Alamitos High, where I ghosted through the hallways, or from my own home, where I acted up just to stay visible.

Many of my new friends were people I met at my aunt and uncle's church, which was an entirely different experience than any I'd had before. Dad had taken our family to church at times—a megachurch that was more concerned with social status than anything else. He tried to give us a spiritual education, but without much of a spiritual education himself, he didn't know how to do it. We were lost. Eventually we quit attending church altogether. But the church Judy and Bill attended, well, it was *warm*—a small country congregation that kept its eyes on heaven instead of on each other's clothes. I liked the feeling of being around so many earnestly devoted people. Unfortunately, it would be a long time before I would find that feeling again.

As autumn steadily approached, it became necessary for me to say goodbye to my farm-fed life and return to Orange County. I said goodbye to my new friends, to my country boyfriend, to the church congregation, and to Aunt Judy and Uncle Bill—fully intending to bring my refreshed personality back home with me to Orange County.

Only when I arrived home did I realize just how difficult that would be.

The simple charms of Escondido couldn't hold in Los Alamitos; returning to my high school was an especially difficult transition. It seemed clouded in negativity. And that's where I made my mistake. Instead of fighting for the good, instead of seeking the simple joys I'd found in Escondido, I gave up and went the other way, embraced the darkness, grew a chip on my shoulder the size of a Hollywood premiere, and went looking for trouble.

And if there's one thing that trouble is *very* good at, it's being found.

I went to the mall and traded my espadrilles for four-inch pumps; then I bought 501 jeans and a bunch of knit shirts with no sleeves, tight tops, and short skirts. I was going for a "Belinda Carlisle" look, and I have to say I rocked it pretty well. Over the summer I'd filled out physically, and the change in my body gave me a power I'd never felt before. I had figurative muscle. And I was about to flex.

When I first pulled up at the mall in the glitter-green dune buggy convertible Dad gave me after I returned from Escondido, girls who wouldn't give me a second look when summer started now looked at my wheels, my tan, my clothes, and my curves, and couldn't wait to invite me to their parties.

And the boys? Well, their eyes told me everything I needed to know.

The first time I took my new look and attitude out for a spin, I followed a bunch of new friends out to the beach, where I drank light beer and kissed a football player named Jesse whom I'd met an hour earlier. The night was a dusty haze, fervent and young, and the next morning I felt like a used dishcloth.

But the youthful *power* I felt—it was like I *was* Belinda Carlisle. I could act the way *she* would act, date the boys *she* would date, make the friends *she* would make. It was 100 percent girl power. I wanted to captivate, and I wanted control over my own life.

One friend who shared my "girl power" instinct was Sylvia, a Mexican girl with beautiful skin, pouty lips, and dangerous green eyes. Sylvia hadn't paid much attention to me the previous school year, but when I came back from Escondido with a new look and a hot car, she was eager to be my friend.

I was eager to be her friend too. Sylvia grew up in Tortilla Flats, the bad part of town, which was worlds away from the sprawling, two-story homes in my neighborhood. Even though Sylvia came from a good Catholic family, her zip code gave her a punk-rock legitimacy I found enthralling. Most days after school we'd take off in my sporty dune buggy to cruise Los Alamitos with the Go-Go's blaring, and on Fridays we'd scour the city for older boys willing to buy us Mickey's malt liquor.

For a girl used to being invisible, it was sublime; everywhere we went we made a scene. It didn't matter anymore that Dad hadn't attended my basketball games or that I hadn't received much attention at home. Now I made my own attention.

Our main juice was on Friday and Saturday nights, when Sylvia, her cousin Connie, and I met at Sylvia's house to match outfits and put on makeup over a soundtrack of Loverboy or Huey Lewis and the News.

Then we'd take off in my convertible, looking for the kinds of parties where the kids' parents were out of town and they weren't supposed to have guests, but they did anyway — hundreds of teenaged crazies who wrecked the beds and soiled the carpets and always broke something nice. Parties where the cops came and we hid out in the backyard under a trampoline or dived over a fence to make our way back to the convertible.

It was all such a blast, and in the beginning, neither Dad nor Chris noticed a change in me at all. Not until it was my turn to throw a party, that is. Then they found out everything real quick.

I was not allowed to have people over at the house when Dad and Chris were away, and before my summer in Escondido, it had never been a problem. Who would I have invited over? But now, since I was going to so many parties, of course I had to throw one myself. It's just how it was — sometimes it's your turn.

Dad and Chris were in Palm Springs with Somara and April (Wayne and I weren't invited) the night I asked about twenty-five people to come over for beer and music. I intended for it to be a small get-together with friends, something easy. But by 11:00 p.m., when over two hundred strangers showed up looking for fun and trouble, things quickly grew out of control.

A strange mix of jocks, preps, freaks, geeks, and streets brewed that evening, and as the hour ticked toward midnight, and the alcohol consumption went through the roof, it happened. A fight broke out over a girl—a fight that swelled into a fifteen-person melee rolling through my living room and out onto our back deck, where one boy was thrown through our kitchen window, and another stuck a five-inch blade into somebody's face.

The whole ordeal was a nightmare, and when Dad and Chris arrived home on Sunday they were ushered right into it. Chris would have to miss work to attend the court hearing, and she was livid. She grew even more upset when she received a call at work from my school telling her I hadn't been in class that day.

I was at home when she phoned me in a rage.

"I'm through with you, Sherry Harris," she said. "I'm done. I can't even say I love you anymore. I don't want you here. You're wrecking our family, and I'm just done."

Hearing the words "I can't say I love you" hurt the worst, though it wasn't a surprise. I didn't have the heart to ask her why no one at our house noticed I actually hadn't been in school for weeks, or whether their apathy might have something to do with my behavior.

I tried to reason with her, but hearing that she didn't love me confirmed all my worst fears—that I was a nuisance, that I was a flunkie, that I was a worthless human being.

It was the final shattering of whatever I'd built up in Escondido. Any shred of hope I had of hanging on to life in Los

Alamitos slipped right through my fingers, and the truth of her feelings seized my body and mind in a painful convulsion.

When I hung up the phone, I didn't want to be Sherry Harris anymore. I didn't want to be alive.

I reached up, opened the oak kitchen cabinet door above my head, and took out a tall drinking glass.

I filled it with water and took it to the downstairs bathroom and quietly locked the door.

The medicine cabinet door squeaked as I took out a brand new bottle of aspirin. Five hundred tablets.

I took the cotton from the top of the jar and shook an entire handful onto my palm and swigged them down. Then I did it again. Then again, over and over until I gagged on the white powder and the bottle was empty.

Then I started to cry. Sylvia had stopped by the house right before Chris called, and I could hear her on the other side of the door asking if I was okay.

I was not okay. Sounds muffled like the inside of a seashell. The room started spinning. I stood up and looked in the mirror. Mascara streaking my face. Pink lipstick still on the drinking glass.

Sylvia banged on the door, and so I opened it, but I was crying too hard to speak.

She saw the empty bottle on the sink.

"Sherry, what have you done?"

She hustled past and turned the aspirin bottle upside down. "Did you take these? Did you? Please tell me you didn't."

I couldn't answer, so she ran downstairs and dialed the operator. Then she called my father at work.

"She's dying!" she screamed into the phone.

"Who is?"

"Your daughter! Sherry! There's no time!"

Then I was floating through the house and into an ambulance, where EMTs filled me with black charcoal until I threw up.

Chapter 4

A Girl Named Tuesday

When Dad rushed out of his office to be with me at the hospital, he was too embarrassed to admit what I'd done, so he told his coworkers that I had a heart problem instead. And in a way, he was more on point that he could possibly know: I *did* have a heart problem. A broken heart.

I was cut off in Orange County, a shadow in my own home. I felt damaged, a relic of a bygone era, like some obsolete computer Dad would throw out at work. And I needed help.

I was released from the hospital the day after I was admitted, and I remember coming home completely unsure of what Dad and Chris thought of me at all. I figured they didn't love me. I didn't love me. Was I expecting too much from them? To like me more than I liked myself?

They didn't say anything about what had happened—not the party, not the hospital, not my grades. Nothing. Maybe they didn't know how to deal with it. Maybe they just didn't care. I didn't care either, but I managed to finish the rest of eleventh grade at Los Alamitos without incident. I kept my head down. The girl who'd returned from Escondido had been washed away by aspirin and neglect. And I didn't know who was left.

My dad decided to pull me out of public high school after the year was up, mainly because I would not have the credits necessary to graduate as a senior. I was nearly two years behind.

He enrolled me in Laurel, a brand new alternative school for troubled youths. At Laurel I could complete enough work to earn a high school certificate.

I'm sure Dad hoped a new school would be the change I so desperately needed, and it certainly started out that way. I enjoyed Laurel. The twenty-nine students in our inaugural class were a motley bunch—new wavers, beatnik wannabes, potheads, hipsters, and kids with bipolar disorder—but we got along well because we all had one thing in common: we'd blown it somewhere else.

I responded well to Laurel's teaching methods, which favored practical, one-on-one learning over rote memorization, and I flourished in my studies. The teachers seemed to truly care, and so I in turn worked hard to make them proud of me. I was even voted class president. It felt good to gain a sense of control.

As class president, my job was to buy snacks for the school, and I vividly remember that it was Dad who took me to Vons grocery store for Little Debbie cakes and chips. It was a special day for me, the only one I can remember in California when Dad and I spent time alone together. That was it, our father-daughter bonding moment: trolling the junk food aisles with a shopping cart and a list, checking off items and me wishing there were more purchases so our trip would last longer.

But even given Laurel's more positive learning environment and my new sense of responsibility, I still failed to control my behavior outside of class. I quickly fell back into old habits; I always had a knack for finding the best keg parties. I came home later and later, often missing my curfew by hours. By the spring semester, Dad and Chris were so fed up with my drinking, my late nights, and my generally poor attitude that they reached a tipping point, angrily deciding that I had to move out of their house once and for all.

For so long I had struggled to be seen by both of them. And

now, after a good look, they'd decided they didn't like what they saw. I'll never forget the moment when my father asked me to which city he should buy my one-way plane ticket. I felt as though I'd failed him—and that he'd failed me too. I had no idea where to go, so I selected St. Petersburg, Florida. My mom lived a half an hour from the airport.

Leaving Orange County wasn't cathartic at all. It seemed routine. Once again Sherry Harris was starting over. I'd done it before and I'd do it again. Starting over was as comfortable to me as an old pair of shoes, and just as with old shoes, it would be a long time before I would realize how much wear and tear was taking place. Bad habits always seem comfortable until you run aground. Old shoes seem fine until they suddenly unravel, and you find yourself walking barefoot over glass.

Mom picked me up at the airport with Frank, her boyfriend, and together we drove into Gulfport, where they co-owned a tiny two-bedroom house. One bedroom was for sleeping, and Frank used the other bedroom as his office. Their compromise for me, if it could be called such, was to erect a cardboard partition between Frank's desk and my sleeping bag. My head rested next to the wastebasket.

Obviously the situation was flawed from the start, and so I wasn't too surprised, just two weeks into our arrangement, when Mom and Frank decided it was better that I stay somewhere else.

"I'm sorry," she told me, "but with his work, Frank really needs his privacy."

"Where am I supposed to go?"

"Don't worry," she said. "I have an idea."

She owned a bookstore on Forty-Ninth Street called "Celebrity Books." Her big idea was to let me sleep there, in the wash closet near the back. The bookstore was located in a rough part of town—gun shops and liquor stores—and I was scared out of my wits the first night I slept there. Mom forbade me from turning on the lights, both to avoid suspicion from local store owners, and to keep from attracting attention from the police. So from 8:00 p.m. to sunup, I cowered in pitch-black horror, listening for things that creep in the night.

I stayed in the bookstore wash closet for seven nights until Mom managed to find other arrangements—a small cottage listed in the classifieds. She picked me up early in the morning, and we drove to an apartment with low ceilings. It smelled stale; the walls were marked by nail holes; it had a nasty roach problem; and it had a front door held together with a loose-fitted latch—but it *was* $150 to move in. So we took it.

Her only condition was that I find a job and begin paying her back immediately. I agreed but did so without considering that I had no idea how to find a job on my own, nor did I know how to keep a job once it was found. So I spent a few hours each day walking up and down the streets of St. Pete asking cashiers for work and looking for "Help Wanted" signs. But there were few jobs in the neighborhood suitable for an underage girl, and even fewer employers interested in a girl who looked like Belinda Carlisle and hadn't finished twelfth grade.

I was so green back then. A seventeen-year-old Sherry Harris had nothing on the survival instincts of an Amish girl, who by seventeen has already mastered cooking, cleaning, and selling homemade goods. I didn't even realize my $150 rent was due *every month*; I thought the first payment bought me at least half a year. So who was "unworldly"—the Amish or me?

I never did find a job during my first month living in the cottage. And then, after one particularly fruitless day, I came home to find my front door padlocked shut.

I banged on the window of my Lithuanian landlord's house.

"Yes?" he said, lumbering up to his screen door.

"Why is my door locked?"

"No rent."

"I did pay rent," I said. "I paid rent when I moved in."

He shook his head. "Idiot girl. That last month. Where this month?"

"This month?"

He nodded. "This month."

I didn't know where "this month" was supposed to come from. I didn't know I even needed "this month." I pleaded with him to give me more time, even a week, but he wouldn't have it. "No rent, no stay" was all he said, over and over.

So I turned around and left.

Most of what I owned was still inside my apartment. The landlord stood over me and allowed me to take only what I could stuff into a blue Guess backpack. Everything else that said who I was or where I'd been—gone forever. The identity of Sherry Harris was now under the management of an angry Lithuanian, and I was a ghost. A no-name.

It wasn't until I reached the street that I realized I had no place to go.

I walked for hours looking for someplace—anyplace—to rest my head. I had little money and no prospects. There was no moon in the sky, and I didn't own a watch, so I had no idea what time it was when I finally curled up on a metal bench near "Casino" dance club. I remember hoping the street lamp overhead would scare away anyone looking to do me harm. Luckily no one bothered me all night.

I never did fall asleep, and as soon as the morning sun peaked over the horizon I rolled off the bench to try to find some food. The morning bread truck was just lumbering by, and I imagined I could smell the hot croissants, rolls, and bagels tucked deep inside—good food for good people. I licked my lips and pined for toothpaste. The sun was already steaming hot overhead, so I wiped my face with a newspaper, fixed my hair in the reflection of a glassed-in bus stop, and headed down to the beach.

I went for an early morning swim and dozed lazily underneath the lifeguard station for the rest of the day. I didn't know it at the time, but I'd unwittingly created a routine I would follow for months afterward: wake at the sound of the bread truck, wash up at the beachside shower, sit on the sand until sunrise, doze under the lifeguard station, and then stay up all night on a metal bench under a flickering street lamp.

I used the last of my money on a bathing suit, a pencil, a notebook, and some Suave Strawberry shampoo at Winn Dixie. The bathing suit and shampoo were so I wouldn't look homeless; the pencil and paper so I wouldn't go insane.

Those early days made for a rough go. A person like me wasn't prepared for this kind of life; I wasn't a survivor. I was from Orange County, and I drove a glitter-green dune buggy my father had bought me with computer money. Every afternoon I stood at a pay phone fighting the urge to call my father. Why didn't I make the call? I don't know—I was embarrassed. I was ashamed. And most of all, I was afraid he wouldn't care.

Looking back on it now, I'm not sure I would've made it at all, if it weren't for a surprising revelation. I was sitting on the beach when it happened.

I was long accustomed to people not seeing me, but when you're homeless, you realize how little *anybody* sees anyone else at all. I guess we don't notice because we're too busy with our own lives and our own thoughts, but when you don't have a life, when you don't have anyone to see or anything to do—that's when you understand: we're all a little invisible.

I was invisible, and as I sat in the sand watching person after person walk by me, with no concern as to who I was or what I was doing, I wondered what I could do to be seen. Sure, I'd left most of my stuff behind with a Lithuanian landlord, but that didn't mean I had to stay a ghost. I just had to change. Adapt.

Hadn't I done the same when I moved to Escondido? That

Sherry was worlds apart from the one in Orange County. Now I just had to do it again. Find a part of myself that was worlds away from the girl who cried to herself every night on a metal bench. I would have to become somebody smart, become a girl who knew all the angles. Somebody tough. Somebody hip and bohemian. Somebody cool.

There was a man who worked near my mom's bookstore who had tried to flirt with me a few weeks before, and in doing so, he'd called me a name that hadn't registered with me then. But now it caught fire in my mind.

Tuesday.

That was what he called me.

Tuesday could be a girl who didn't care what people thought of her. She could be confident and tough. She could walk into a bar, chat up some guy, and get him to buy her a meal, even if there was a price to pay later. And once I jotted these thoughts down in my notebook, once I wrote down in ink what I was about to write into life, I went ahead and took my new "cover" out for a spin on a Friday night.

The effect was nothing short of remarkable.

Tuesday had a much easier time sticking up for herself. Tuesday told scummy guys to get lost. She was a girl who knew how to get things done, an invincible youth wise beyond her years.

I was a little girl playing dress up. And I have to admit—I liked how I looked.

Beach kids started asking me to come home with them for meals, and I accepted every invitation I could. At night I went to backyard parties, and when the lovers began to sneak away, and the barbeque died out, I'd excuse myself with a stomach full of hamburgers. Then I'd creep back to the corner of Beach and Shore Boulevard alone, to my metal bench under the stars.

I slept on the street for almost six months all told, and while the power I got from Tuesday helped me survive, I never forgot where I was and what happens to people who stay there too long. All streets eventually dead-end, after all, and if you're barreling down a dead-end street, then the end eventually comes for you too.

Sometimes I'd follow people I barely knew back to crummy apartments, where strangers shot heroin; I'd hop into any car that offered a ride going anywhere; I'd end up alone with strange men at strange parties in strange areas of a city that came darkly alive at night.

Those moments don't always turn out so well. And it crossed my mind that if I disappeared—what then? My family would never know what happened. I hadn't spoken with them in months. Nobody on earth had a clue where I was, and my beachside friends knew me as Tuesday. How long would I remain missing before my dad found out? Maybe I would just fade into the wind, my face a haunting profile: "MISSING—some girl named Tuesday."

There were a million possibilities, each one scarier than the next, and those possibilities formed a countdown of sorts in my head, a ticking life-bomb that could explode at any time. I just had a feeling that soon something would give, something wicked would come. And when it came not even Tuesday could save me.

"Sherry?"

I hadn't heard that name in months.

One of my girlfriends rolled over on her beach towel. "Tuesday, do you know this lady?"

I cupped my hand over my eyes, and suddenly that ticking clock in my head grew much louder. It was my cousin Judy, who was eight years older than me and a favorite. Judy, who'd babysat Wayne and me when we were little.

"Uh … yeah. Hold on," I said, and hopped up. Then I hooked Judy's arm and led her away.

"Sherry, what's—"

"Wait."

At the lifeguard stand, Judy pulled her arm from mine and stopped.

"Sherry, what is going on?"

I squeezed my hands, unsure where to start. "How did you find me?"

"I don't know ..." She looked frazzled. "I haven't heard from you. I thought you might be here at the beach. I've been looking for you ... I ... I asked around, and the lifeguard said he'd seen a blond girl out here every day for weeks ... so I just walked down the beach, and ..."

"Here I am."

"Here you are."

"Listen, Judy, it's nice to see you, but—"

"Sherry where are you living?"

I kicked at the sand. "I don't know. Around."

"Where's around?"

"You know, here and there."

It was clear she wasn't going to let me go without answers. "Why did that girl call you Tuesday?"

I shrugged. "She's confused or something."

Judy was smart, and she was a mother, and so she wasn't about to fall for any of my nonsense. She grabbed my arm hard—like a mother does when she senses trouble.

"Sherry Harris, you tell me right now what's going on."

I didn't want to tell her anything. But hearing my full name for the first time in months wrenched something free, because in an instant Tuesday fell away and it was just me again, Sherry Harris, standing alone on the beach and blinking into the sun.

"I ... I ..." The words were hard to say.

"Are you on drugs?"

"No. I'm just ..."

"What?"

"What!" she said again, squeezing my arm. "Sherry, listen to me. I am your cousin and I love you." She jerked me closer to her face. "You're going to tell me where you've been. Right now. Here. Understand?"

"Yes."

"Where do you live?"

"Nowhere."

"Where do you sleep?"

"On a bench."

"What bench?"

"The one across the street."

"In *this* neighborhood?"

"Yes."

This she wasn't expecting. "Sherry ... what? I don't understand."

"I don't either." I'd spent so much time worrying about the people who never saw me, that I'd forgotten the people in my life, like Judy, who always had.

"Honey, are you living out here?" Her arm slackened and she moved closer.

"Yes."

"But why?"

Her question was simple, but it allowed me to see my situation clearly for the first time in months. I was tired and sick and lonely. This wasn't some bohemian adventure Tuesday cooked up; this was a crisis—of family, of home, of belonging—that left me alone on the street.

I started to cry.

"I'm just really, really sad, Judy. And I'm really scared. And I have nowhere else to go."

"Oh, Sherry ..." Her fury broke and she pulled me deep into

her chest. Then she put her lips close to my ear and whispered softly, "Go tell your friends goodbye and get your things. You're coming home with me."

Home. I didn't know what the word meant anymore. But I knew I wanted what it stood for—more than I could say.

Judy lived in Pinellas Park with her husband, Pat, and their three little girls. Theirs was a stable and healthy home, full of good cheer and faith, and they offered me a place to stay for a couple of months while I attempted to get back on my feet.

They were a devout Christian family—quite a reversal from my life on the streets. And just like in Escondido, I marveled at how seriously they took the Word of God. It seemed to give them an inner light.

Pat read passages from the Bible over breakfast each morning. Judy lulled her children to sleep with Bible stories. Jennifer and Patricia, ages five and three-and-a-half, sang along to sweet Christian songs on a tape recorder and even let me join in.

For a short time I even attended First Baptist Church at Indian Rocks with Judy's family, and I found that I quickly slipped into the same spirit of grace I'd experienced in Escondido. It was an expectant feeling, as if someone had been waiting for me for a long time. Or maybe calling me to come back.

But I didn't listen. I never listened. And I enjoyed my wild clothes, wild hair, wild music, and wild boys. Those were earthly delights I could not give up, and I assumed God would not love me until I did. I had no idea He could accept the person I was then, that He could love her. See her. I certainly couldn't do those things myself. Like the people who'd walked by me on the beach, I couldn't see me at all.

I left Judy and Pat's house about six weeks after I arrived. They offered me a longer stay, but I declined—I was desperate to be on my own again. To their credit, Judy and Pat understood the agitations of a young and restless girl—we've all been teenagers—but they weren't about to let me walk right back out into the street with no prospects and no plan.

Pat sat me down and explained what sort of employers might hire someone with my meager qualifications, and he showed me which neighborhoods to avoid and how to use the classified ads. Judy gave me a crash course in the sort of motherly advice I'd never received, teaching me to stand up straight, speak clearly, and look people in the eyes when I spoke. She also bought me a cute lavender dress for my job interviews.

Armed with their advice and my new dress, I soon landed a job at the Hurricane Restaurant—a hip, two-story seafood place on Pass-a-Grille Beach. The pay was enough that I could afford my own apartment, and so a couple of weeks after leaving Judy's house, I spread the classifieds over a motel floor, sat down with a landline phone, and worked through each listing in the "Roommate Wanted" section.

Most of the listings were obvious scams, but one apartment by the bay looked promising. I took a deep breath and dialed the number on the ad.

"Hello?" answered a sweet voice.

"Um ... yeah, I'm calling about the apartment?"

"Well, you got the right girl. I'm looking for one person and no drama."

"I'm no drama."

"I'll take your word for it. Listen—it's not a great place, but it's downtown, close to everything, and the rent's cheap. I'm easygoing, and so I'm not looking for any trouble. Are you trouble?"

"Usually not."

"Ha! At least you're honest. When would you wanna move in?"

"Today."

"Well, good, 'cause I need somebody yesterday. Look, why don't you come over and see the place? I'll be here for a couple of hours. If you like it and we get along you can move in whenever you want."

She just had one more question.

"What's your name?"

I took a second to consider. Who was I, really?

"Tuesday. My name's Tuesday."

"Are you serious?"

"Yes ... I ..."

"Hey listen, you don't have to explain. This may sound crazy—"

"What?"

"My name's Sunday. And I can't wait to meet you."

Sunday really was her name, and when we met up a few hours later we got along like old friends. She was from Miramar, near Miami, and she was in St. Petersburg attending college. She was only eighteen years old but already a junior, because she'd graduated high school a few years early—a real brainiac. I moved into her attic bedroom later that same night.

Sunday and I had more fun living together than I'd had in just about any other time in my life. She was a curvy Italian girl with dyed red hair who loved going to clubs and drove the men wild on the dance floor. Neither one of us was old enough to get into bars legally, so she used an older person's driver's license, while I used a fake ID that said my name was "Tanya Composto" and that I was twenty-two years old. Once again I could be someone else, someone other than Sherry Harris—even if just for a few hours on Saturday night.

Every weekend we hit the dance clubs under our assumed names, and then, every Monday, we reverted to our normal selves: Tuesday heading off to work, Sunday off to class. Sunday insisted we keep our weekend and weekday selves separate. She had plans for her life, and I learned a lot from her in that respect. It wasn't too long before her studious habits were even rubbing off on me a little. Could I get my high school diploma? Could I attend college someday?

When Sunday's semester ended, however, she decided to move home and give up the apartment we shared. Her parents felt bad about the sudden change and offered to help me — but I was sick of Florida. I hadn't lived in one spot longer than a couple of months during my entire stay in the sunshine state.

So instead of paying for an apartment, I asked Sunday's mother if she would mind loaning me $150 for a plane ticket to California instead. Watching Sunday attack her studies day after day had given me encouragement. I wanted to set some goals for myself, work hard for once, and maybe even seek out a few dreams of my own.

I knew I could do those things in California. For California is in the business of making dreams come true.

Chapter 5

CAN YOU PLAY A SONG FOR MY FRIEND?

If you put a photo of my young, restless self next to a photo of me taken today, you might not realize it's the same person. I'm not even sure I would recognize myself.

It was the 1980s—years after my stint living on the beach—and I was twenty-two, blond, and worlds away from a head covering.

Things were looking up for Sherry Harris. I rented a hip apartment on the beach in Surfside and deejayed at night. The deejay job was serendipitous; I'd been hired at a skating rink as an instructor, but when the owners found out how much I knew about popular music, they quickly ushered me up to the announcer's booth and put a mic in my hand. I'd left that first job for a place called Skate Depot, and it was there—amid the colored lights, the vinyl, all that sound and motion—that I found my true calling.

I loved watching those kids fly 'round and 'round the oval in perfect sync with the records spinning in my booth. I loved working with children. I loved getting paid for talking. And I loved running the show. I knew which records to play and when, how to slow things down for the couples, and then how to crank the mood back up again with the newest hit single and a blast of strobing light.

I was comfortable on the microphone, confident, and in control. I'd been getting extra practice on local college radio. A friend of mine ran the station, and after I'd pestered him about it for weeks, he'd agreed to let me take a swing at an afternoon top-40 show broadcast over the school loudspeakers. It was an instant hit around campus.

I was homeless, friendless, clueless no more. My radio shows aired twice a week, Tuesdays and Thursdays. I saved up my deejay money and bought a Yamaha YSR motorcycle for a thousand dollars. And my boyfriend was as wild as I was — a film stuntman and professional freestyle BMX rider who was rated number 1 in the world. Together, he and I raced through Los Alamitos and Long Beach in his white Porsche, listening to the freshest cuts from the hottest radio station, Power 106 FM.

I was living a California dream.

Power 106 FM would play an important role in my life. One morning I was listening to *Morning Zoo*, a popular drive-time radio show hosted by Jay Thomas and Monica Brooks. Jay — who would find stardom on *Cheers*, *Love and War*, and *Murphy Brown* — was talking about hiring a new on-air personality. Apparently, "Powermouth Patty" had left the show.

Deejaying on Los Angeles radio seemed like the coolest job in the world to me, way cooler than working the announcing booth at a skating rink. At that particular moment in my life, I was so flush with confidence that I thought, "You know what? I'm going to march right down to that station and get that on-air job this minute."

So I wiggled my way into a tight dress and raced into downtown Los Angeles. I only had a map and an address, so I drove up and down dark streets until I found my way. In the parking lot I found a large set of oak double doors and gave them a hard pull.

They were unlocked.

The hallway inside was upscale and clean, and I took a few false turns before locating the studio window. Then I saw them—Jay and Monica, chatting through a commercial break. I placed my palms flat on the glass and watched in awe; it didn't take long for the two of them to notice me standing in the window.

"Can I help you?" Jay asked.

I opened the door just a crack. "Well,... yes sir. I'm Sherry Harris and I want a job here."

"You do, huh? What kind of job?"

"Disc jockey for *Morning Zoo*." I thought a little spunk might go a long way.

"Oh, you want to sit here? Next to me?" He was having fun with this. "Well, do you have any experience?"

"I deejay at the Skate Depot."

"The Skate Depot."

"Yep. Best one there."

"I see." His eyes widened. "Oh, I know! Listen, here's what we'll do. Sherry, you stand here next to me, and when we come back live, you're going to pretend that you just walked in. Then I'm going to pretend to think you're a stripper sent here as a prank. You understand?"

"Jay—I'm a pro. I get it."

His eyebrows nearly flew off his head. "A pro! You hear, Monica? Sherry already knows the lingo!"

He laughed again, and at that moment the lights on the board flashed, signaling we were about to go on-air. I took a deep breath. This could be my big break. Jay turned back to the mic as easily as someone would pick up a phone call, even though he was speaking to almost two million listeners.

"Hey, we're back at Power 106, and I just gotta say ... things got a little weird during the break. Apparently there's been a mix-up or something because we got a girl here — what's your name, honey?"

I leaned forward and spoke into the mic. "Sherry Harris, Mr. Thomas."

"Mr. Thomas?" He brightened. "I like that." He turned to Monica. "You see how I should be treated around here?"

Monica said, "It's just because she doesn't know you yet."

He shook his head. "You don't appreciate me. But you — " he turned back to me — "Sherry Harris ... let's see ... you're *not* a stripper, right?"

"Pretty sure of it."

"But when you walked in ... I'm so sorry, but I thought what I thought. You all gotta see Sherry here — beautiful girl. But that was my mistake. You forgive me?"

"Anything for you, Jay."

"I see we're already past 'Mr. Thomas.' But Sherry, here's what I don't understand — if you're *not* a girl sent down here by some prankster, then what is it you want?"

"I'm a disc jockey."

"Yes?"

"And I think you should hire me."

Jay laughed again, and then he asked me about my career, and for the next three minutes of my life, two million people in the greater Los Angeles area heard me banter back and forth with Jay Thomas and Monica Brooks. I was on top of the world. He even let me sign off with an ad-libbed, open-mic promo: "So come on down and see me, Sherry Harris, rocking the booth at Skate Depot — the same fresh new music mix as Power 106!"

Jay escorted me out at the commercial break, putting a kind hand on my shoulder.

"Sherry, you did great. You're a natural. Now, are you serious about getting a job? Or did you come down here on a dare or something?"

"I'm serious."

"Even if it's something unpaid or entry-level and not on-air?"

"Yes, sir."

"Okay," he nodded, and then pointed down the hallway. "Go down this hall and take your first right. That's Howard's office—he's the station manager. Tell him Jay sent you."

"Really?"

"Really. I like to look out for the young people. Just don't take my job, okay?"

"I promise." From homeless girl to possibly working with Jay Thomas, a personal hero. I'd come so far in such a short time.

Once I'd said my goodbyes to Jay, I nearly skipped down the station hallway, passing Pam Dawber of *Mork and Mindy* fame, and wheeled into a cluttered office, where I found Howard sifting papers behind an oak desk.

He looked up. "Yes?"

"Jay Thomas sent me here. He said you could give me a job."

"What kind of job?"

"I don't know. A disc jockey job."

"A deejay? Do you have an agent?"

"No."

"An FCC license?"

I shook my head.

He leaned back in his chair and smiled. "Oh—you must be the girl who walked in off the street."

"That's me."

"Ha! That was about the gutsiest thing I've ever heard. What's your name?"

"Sherry Harris, sir."

"Well, Sherry Harris, I like your attitude. Now, the reality is that I can't make you a deejay out of the blue. You need an awful lot of experience and an FCC license. But I'm impressed with the work you did today, and so I'm going to give you a shot. We have a show called *Hotspots* that runs on Saturday nights. Do you know the show?"

"I don't."

"Well, that's okay—it's not for everybody. But we use it to develop new talent for the station, so why don't you give it a listen, and then if it seems like something you'd be interested in, you call me back, and I'll see if I can get you on board. Deal?"

"Deal!" I said brightly.

"Okay, then maybe I'll be seeing you around. But please don't make a habit of showing up on-air without notice."

"Yes, sir," I said. Then we shook hands and I left.

I felt high as a kite on my way home from the station. Could this be the opportunity that would change my life? But then, later on in the week, when I listened to the *Hotspots* segment for the first time, I learned my "golden ticket" was anything but.

Hotspots, as it turned out, was a radio show about the greater Los Angeles club scene, with on-air girls reporting the latest gossip. I knew instantly that I wasn't right for the job. Maybe two years ago I was, when Sunday and I tore up dance floors in south Florida, or even five years ago, when Sylvia and I raced from party to party in my green dune buggy.

But not now. Not as I was trying desperately to avoid my past mistakes. Tuesday hadn't worked out so well for me, and I was only recently starting to learn about Sherry Harris. It would be a shame to forget her again so quickly.

So I called Howard back and I told him that I wasn't right for the job. He understood. He told me to keep at it, though, to keep working hard at my craft. He even said that if I got some experience down the line, I should call him back and maybe we could work something out.

I was disappointed after I hung up the phone; I felt like I'd let him down. But it was the right thing to do, and I was proud I'd had the gumption to drive to the radio station in the first place.

I would just have to create another opportunity for myself, I figured—one that was more in line with the person I was slowly becoming. I would focus even harder on the work I *did* have, and become the best disc jockey I could be.

And in the next few months that's exactly what I did.

More and more people lined up for my shift on Friday and Saturday nights at the rink, and the more the lines lengthened, the harder I tried. I was living in Los Angeles, after all. And in LA, the right person could literally make a career overnight.

Ironically, it wasn't during a hot Saturday night when my first real opportunity walked through the door; but a super-slow Sunday instead, with hardly twenty people at the rink. And one of them was about to hand me the golden ticket I'd been looking for.

We were closing up and my shift had just ended. As I tidied the sound booth, a friend dropped by to hand me a business card.

"It's from a guy I know," said my friend. "I told him about your work here, and he said to give him a call."

I slipped the card in my pocket without giving it another thought. I knew what happened when a girl got her hopes up. In fact, I forgot all about the card until the next afternoon, when I saw it lying face-up on my dresser. "Billy the Kid" was etched into heavy card stock.

"Who would use that name?" I asked myself. That question alone was worth a call, and so I dialed the number.

"Billy," said the voice on the other end.

"Hi, uh, this is Sherry Harris. My friend at—"

"The Skate Depot deejay!" He said suddenly. Apparently my friend had really talked me up.

"Our mutual friend says you have a lot of spunk," Billy said.

This guy sounded like he was fishing for a date.

"Listen, mister, I've got to get to work."

"Wait ... hear me out. My name is Billy, and I work for Fred Segal."

"Who?"

He laughed. "Fred Segal's a company. A retailer. Sells high-end clothes in Santa Monica. They're kind of a big deal."

"And your point is?"

"Well, that's why I wanted to talk with you. I manage the disc jockeys that Fred Segal employs in its store. Right now we have an opening, and I'm looking for a new personality. My friend says you've got a lot of talent. So what do you say? Want to come down to the store and give it a try?"

I couldn't believe what he was saying. "Um ... so are you offering me a job right now?"

"Well, if you want it."

He didn't have to ask me twice.

The Fred Segal job paid three times what I made elsewhere to stand in a Plexiglas sound booth and spin records. It was a cinch. Occasionally I announced a sale, but most of the time I played whatever top-40 hits I wanted to hear or took requests from the customers.

And these weren't just any customers.

Movie stars came in regularly, for Fred Segal catered almost exclusively to celebrities. It was a safe haven where they could shop like regular people, without being hassled, because the prices were so astronomical that no potential hasslers could afford anything in the store.

Literally every shopper was famous, which brought them a sense of privacy. It wasn't like Sting was going to ask Cher to sign his baseball cap.

There were only two rules for us employees: Never ask for an autograph, and *never* play a Jermaine Jackson song if Michael was in the store. Now, I never got the backstory on Michael's beef with Jermaine, but as for not hounding people for autographs, I was fine with that. I never much worshiped celebrities anyway.

But there was one day I did have an interesting moment with someone I liked very much.

It occurred when a slim and very handsome man walked in with a woman in an expensive, powder-blue pantsuit. The man drifted to the back of the store, while the woman walked over to my booth.

I took off my headphones. "Can I help you?"

"I hope so," she said. "Can you play a song for my friend?"

"Sure. What does he want?"

"*Midnight Train to Georgia* by Gladys Knight and the Pips."

"Will do," I said.

I dug through our vast collection of records. I knew we had the song, but as I searched the "G's" I just couldn't find it. Then I searched the "P's" for "Pips"—also nothing. As I continued to look, I threw on a record from the band Exposé.

When I next glanced up from our records, the handsome man was standing just outside my booth shaking his head.

"Now, that's not *Midnight Train to Georgia*, I don't think."

I suddenly recognized him. It was none other than Rob Lowe. *St. Elmo's Fire* had just come out in the theatres, and every girl in America knew his name.

"I know, I'm so sorry. I couldn't find it."

He shook his head. "It's okay. But it's a great song. You guys need to have it." He winked at me. "For next time, okay?"

"Sure."

I beamed for the rest of that day and the next. Imagine meeting Rob Lowe! And it wasn't just him; every big name in Hollywood stopped by our store. With so many influential people coming in and out of Fred Segal every day, I just *knew* it was only a matter of time before I scored my big break. I could already see the rags-to-riches headline in *People* magazine: "Formerly Homeless Woman Becomes Disc Jockey Superstar."

My destiny was to have a big career. It would be my salvation. It would silence my naysayers and show my family I had worth.

Sure, Sherry Harris had always been second place in her own home. But one day, when she was a superstar, she would be first place with everyone else.

Chapter 6

A QUICK NOTE

A professional career. Material possessions. Respect and admiration.

For a long time, I believed those concepts could fill the hole in my heart left when my parents withdrew their love. I had faith in those concepts, faith they could lift me up and save me from myself. But there is only one type of faith able to change a person, and unfortunately it would still be a long time until I found that out firsthand.

What I did find, and rather quickly I might add, was that faith in desire—for fame, for respect—only works when times are good. Then they can make you feel invulnerable. At Fred Segal I charged ahead, full of steam and gumption, like I was about to tackle the whole world.

But then life reminded me—again—why it can be so hard. And when the skies darkened overhead, when I needed something to brace myself upon, where was my misguided faith in ambition?

Crumbling into the dust, just like everything else.

I'm going to be honest with you. This is difficult. There is a part of my life that for many years was largely unopened, even to me. It was a drawn window shade. A storefront with the metal awning pulled down. I didn't talk about it, and I didn't think about it.

But this is my story, and this is what stories do: they tell things you don't want heard so that somebody else may find peace. So here goes.

When I was eighteen, before Skate Depot and Fred Segal and my Yamaha motorcycle, I had an abortion with a boy I'd known since high school. When I found out I was with child, the pressure from all sides was intense. Back then, rich girls in Orange County didn't have children out of wedlock, or at least none that I knew of. It was considered low-class. Everybody said it was no big deal. They said it was just "a little blob of tissue." I sought help at various places around town, but most organizations could only provide services until the child was born. After that I'd be on my own. And I was so young.

I wanted to be a mother, but I was terrified of ending up homeless again. "Don't ruin your life," people said to me. "You're too immature for this." "Think of what you're throwing away."

So I made a choice to end the pregnancy.

But then, not too long after I took my job at Fred Segal, not too long after I'd decided on a lasting career as a disc jockey, I became with child for the second time. And for the second time I made the same decision.

It was a decision, like the first, made purely in self-interest. And that is why I suffered afterward—why I so swiftly transformed from an ambitious girl to someone overcome with grief. I felt as if I was standing under a sagging umbrella in a driving rain, puddles everywhere at my feet. I felt as if I'd made the biggest mistake of my life.

And everything I'd built for myself disappeared in an instant.

I quit going to work. Quit seeing my friends. Fred Segal? Gone. Skate Depot? Gone. College radio? Gone. I moved out of one apartment and into another and then moved again. The world around me shrank to the size of a pea. I hit rock bottom, a dark place with traumas too horrible to mention. Everything was over. Everything had fallen apart.

I never want to relive those days, but it would be foolhardy to forget them. And it would be disingenuous to deny what they meant.

I've learned the hard way what it costs to live for yourself. I was broken and empty, but even then, I sensed I was being called to look away from the material, to look away from the self, as the source of fulfillment.

I had assumed my life would be a certain way. Then it was leveled. And only then did I realize there was another path at my feet.

Chapter 7

ALL FOR HER

It took me a long time to come back from the darkness.

I received intense counseling at Didi Hirsch Mental Health Services, and though I wasn't diagnosed with clinical depression, my counselors referred to my state as a "worried well"—meaning I was constantly worried about not being well. It was plain that I was acutely and chronically sad.

When I left the center, I knew it was going to be a long and slow trudge back to normalcy, and it was difficult for me to conceive of doing so in Southern California. I'd tossed away my opportunities. California seemed as dark as it had when I'd first returned from Escondido years earlier. I still needed relief. I still needed an escape.

And once I began looking for an escape, I found it in the most surprising of places: a movie theatre.

A friend of mine, Gary, took me to see a movie called *Good Morning, Vietnam*, starring Robin Williams as Adrian Cronauer, a disc jockey in the middle of the Vietnam War. The film was open and honest about the tragic nature of war, but as I watched the story unfold, I found I was thoroughly taken by the idea of armed service. It was honorable. It was stable. It took people out of their own worlds and placed them in another.

It was an escape. And that's when I conceived of a way to get out of California: Sherry Harris could join the Army.

Today, I live amongst the Plain people, many of them strident pacifists. The ideal of nonresistance is deeply rooted in Amish and Mennonite culture. I'm not all the way there myself, for I would protect my children at any cost, but it's still a big jump to think that decades ago, Gary and I marched down to an army field office and signed up without a second thought.

I took the ASVAB—the Army's aptitude test—wondering if I could score high enough to enlist, and I passed on my first try. My verbal scores were very good and my math scores very poor—so poor, in fact, that the discrepancy fell well outside of the norm. The officials asked that I take the test for a second time, and though I scored even higher, my verbal and math scores were still at odds. I told the officers that I'd always struggled with numbers, and they suggested I might have a deficit in math, a diagnosis confirmed years later through counseling. It felt good to hear my math problems might be the result of a disorder. Maybe I wasn't "just a flunkie" as my father had diagnosed so many years before.

Once my ASVAB test was certified, I moved through the enlistment process quickly and was sworn in as a cadet. It was then time to learn which army position the ASVAB said I was most suited for. When I first saw the results my jaw hit the floor.

Missile launcher.

That's right—the same woman who can often be found sitting in a simple dress in front of Big Olaf Ice Cream in Pinecraft was, at one time, appointed to launch missiles.

In a way, the test was spot on—back then I was launching missiles against myself and those I blamed for my circumstances all the time.

I was told to report to boot camp in North Carolina in three months' time, and I decided to take a break from California. I hadn't spent much time with Cousin Judy or her family in a long while—not since I'd lived with them briefly—and so I bought a bus ticket to Florida to say goodbye before I joined the military for good.

Judy, Pat, their children, and I picked up right where we'd left off years before, spending a few wonderful days together. It was so much fun that I began to dread my return for boot camp and the four-year commitment to the army it would entail. I have to admit that I panicked a little. I'd wanted to escape California, and I'd planned to do it via the military, but now I was in Florida enjoying myself with California already behind me. It begged the question: Did I really want to shoot missiles at other people for the rest of my life? And did I really want to live in a squat barrack?

In the end I decided no, I did not. So I didn't go back. I stayed in Florida with Judy and got a job instead, found a place to live near their neighborhood.

Today it's bizarre to think about, but for twenty years I thought there might still be a listing somewhere, deep in the United States Army Archives, with my name on it: "Sherry Harris, Missile Launcher—AWOL." Thankfully, I've since learned a person must be sworn in twice.

In Florida I began to heal some of the wounds that had knocked me so dreadfully off course in California. Judy's family reinforced a new outlook I was beginning to develop, one focused on settling down and starting a family. My brief focus on career had ended disastrously. It was time for me to grow up, become an adult, and finally embrace the things that really mattered.

It was in that frame of mind, then, that I first met Darren Gore. I was working at another skating rink—in the '80s there seemed to be one on every block—when I first caught him making eyes at me from the concession stand. He was tall and blond, and when he walked over and asked if I would like to share a soda with him after work, I said yes.

Later we shared our soda like a couple of young kids, laughing and sharing stories from our lives. I told him I hadn't dated anyone seriously since I'd been in Florida, and he confided that he'd never really had a long-term girlfriend. I think that's why I took to him so fast. He seemed desperate for the same things I was: a little stability, a little home cooking, and a little slice of the American dream.

We had our first date a week after, a pleasant evening of dinner and a movie. He kept me in stitches for most of the night, for Darren had a real talent for making light of other people. He could just watch a person pass, make a comment, and I'd nearly drop to the floor in a fit.

Later on during that first date, however, he said something that wasn't so funny at all.

"I want a family," he said, after I'd asked him what he wanted out of life. "I just want to find someone to settle down with. Somebody to give me a child."

A child. It seemed he heard the same ticking biological clock I was just starting to hear. I had a hole in my heart the size of the moon, and now here came Darren Gore, a shovel in his hands, promising to fill it up. I was smitten.

Our young relationship progressed rather quickly, and within a couple of months we'd already pooled enough money to rent a small bungalow on Lido Beach. It was a decision I would not condone today, since we were not married, but at the time it felt like an enormously positive step. Our plan was simple: move in, get married, have children, and live happily ever after. Funny how it never really turns out that way.

Darren could be a charmer, but he wasn't without his fair share of eccentricities. His mother had to call him every morning to make sure he got up for work. She also called him every night to make sure he'd eaten dinner.

This was odd, but fine at first, until I noticed something. Whenever I attempted to make plans with Darren, he ran it by his mother first.

I guess other women might've seen that as a flashing red light, but I couldn't get upset with Darren about anything; when I looked into his eyes I could see the face of our future child staring right back at me. If I were to get upset with Darren, I would have to get upset with that child too.

We'd hardly been together for three months when we decided to get married, and we didn't wait around to set a date either. We decided on March 18 and chose to hold the ceremony on the beach near our house on Lido Key. I made all of the invitations by hand and even sent one to my father, though I knew he wouldn't be able to come. I purposely picked a date my parents weren't available. Chris was involved with her own sister's wedding, which, as a huge and ornate affair, would invite unfavorable comparisons to the low-key ceremony I was planning.

Even as an adult, I was still afraid my father wouldn't think I was good enough.

Darren and I had little money to spend on the actual ceremony, so I bought an awning at Big Lots and decorated it with cheap plastic flower garlands and drapes. His mother gave me a veil to wear, a graceful gesture on her part, and I found a lovely sarong to wear over my swimsuit. A bride in a two-piece bikini—you won't find that in an Amish neighborhood.

When the morning of our big event arrived, I woke up early and placed two brightly colored sand pails on the beach to mark the spot where Darren's family were to erect the awning while I readied my makeup and hair. It took me thirty minutes to fix myself up, and when I was finished, I stood in front of the mirror and fingered a piece of white lace I'd tied to my sarong. In less than an hour I would become Sherry Gore. I hoped it would be the last transformation I would ever have to make.

Then at 11:00 a.m. sharp it was time. I left my house and walked down a beachside path to the spot I'd staked out in the sand, but nobody was there. Mystified, I looked up and down the coast—nothing. I started back to the house, and then, right when I turned around, I finally saw what I was looking for.

And it didn't look good.

My awning was pitched near the parking lot, right next to the Food Shack. Tourists stuffed their faces with hot dogs and nachos at picnic tables not ten feet away. Cigarette butts littered the white sand. The potluck food we'd asked our guests to bring was spread over two concession tables—without tablecloths— the wood covered in bird droppings.

I will never forget the moment I emerged from the beach and into that mess of a wedding. Beachgoers gawked at me as if I were the trash littering the ground, rather than a bride on her finest day. I covered my face to hide my embarrassment.

Then I looked over our beleaguered wedding attendees. Darren's entire family was there. His aunt had even flown in from Indiana. But my side of the aisle was nearly empty. My friends hadn't come because they disliked Darren and couldn't support my decision to marry him. They'd given me an ultimatum: Darren or them, and I'd chosen Darren. Even my cousin Judy—my maid of honor—had called the night before to say she couldn't make it. She too disliked my fiancé. Only my brother, Wayne—who'd been out on the road for years—had showed up to lend his support.

The justice of the peace waved me forward, and Darren took my hand. I was so shell-shocked walking down the aisle I only dimly perceived the mangy bushes and aluminum trash cans at my side. The whole thing was surreal. Was I really getting married? I glanced at my clothes. Why was I in a bikini? I looked at Darren. Did I really love this man?

The justice raced through her script, and then I watched, completely dazed, as Darren slipped a ring on my finger. I put a ring on his. Then we said our vows, and not two minutes after

I'd first walked into the parking lot, Darren was kissing me and it was all over.

Sherry Harris was no more. Now I was Sherry Gore, for better—or for worse.

Only much later did I learn that Darren's family had moved our ceremony from the beach to the Food Shack because Darren's uncle, who was in a wheelchair, had trouble getting out to the site I'd picked. But instead of just finding a way to carry Darren's uncle to the ceremony, they'd carried the ceremony to Darren's uncle—a choice that foreshadowed my married life with Darren. He was always making choices about my life without asking me first.

It's nothing new to observe that some women find wonderful fiancés that turn into poor husbands right after the wedding. Some men drop the pretense of romance after rings are exchanged; some grow lazy in their affection.

But sometimes it's more than that. Sometimes two people make a promise that only one of them intends to keep.

Darren had promised me he was tired of playing games, that he wanted to bypass the dramatics of young love and settle down, start a family. That he wanted us to be truthful with each other. But he wasn't truthful. As I would soon learn, everything was a game to him. Everything a manipulation.

Con men call it a "bait and switch," and the concept is as old as Adam and Eve: offer a target what they want, get them to sign on the dotted line, and then reveal that they signed up for something else entirely—something they didn't want at all.

Darren had been smart. He'd kept me laughing so hard and for so long that I hadn't noticed the nasty streak hidden beneath his charm. At first the changes were small. For instance, if he found me reading a book, he would sit directly across the room and stare until I couldn't concentrate. Or he'd eat off my plate at restaurants, even after I told him it bothered me.

But then, just weeks into our new life together, I saw a side of him I'd never seen before. We'd gotten into an argument, during which he'd suddenly screamed, "We're *married*! That means I *own* you!"

Then I understood. He thought I was supposed to be like his doting mother—catering to his every wish. And when I demurred, when I expressed displeasure at being his personal plaything, he began a subtle regimen of emotional abuse.

We'd go to the mall and he'd make mooing sounds from behind me, or we'd drive to a 7-Eleven and he'd bellow nonsense until the manager asked us to leave. At night I began jolting awake with shooting pain in my side, certain I'd been pinched. He started leaping out at me from dark corners, scaring me to tears. The more frightened I was the harder he laughed.

They were small humiliations, but over time they added up to something much larger, a single-minded and sinister purpose. Darren was sending me a message: "I own you, and I can do to you what I wish."

But despite all these things, despite the humiliation and disrespect, I was tied to him. I was tied by our wedding vows. I was tied by my need for a traditional life. And about five months after our wedding day, I found I was tied to him by something else, something wonderful—I was going to have a baby.

I was lying in bed next to Darren nine months later when he said something so outrageously funny that I laughed until my water broke. We both jumped out of bed, and I waddled to the front lawn while Darren called his mother. Five minutes later we were on our way.

In the hospital everything was a blur: bright lights and a long corridor, then a bed and nurses feverishly checking my vitals. At first Darren and his mother stayed at my side, but when my baby's heart rate began to drop, the nurse ordered everyone out, and a moment later I was being wheeled down another long corridor, the lights chanting ... *Danger* ... *Danger* ... as they passed overhead.

"What's wrong?" I asked. "What's wrong with my baby?"

"We're going to do an emergency C-section. Don't worry. Just stay calm and breathe."

The smooth curve of the operating room ceiling opened above. I felt the sharp twinge of a needle in my arm. The room started to spin and I blinked. Then everything went dark.

Chapter 8

THE LONG CON

A soft whine like a tiny toy car engine.

"There ... there ... good, right like that—"

And then a roar like a tiger.

I opened my eyes and found a nurse holding something soft and pink in a white cloth.

"Hey there, welcome back," she said. "Look here—look what we've got."

She leaned over and placed a little pink bundle on my chest.

"Just put your arms around her. Yeah, that's good, right like that. This is your daughter, Sherry. Say hello."

I looked down at Jacinda Michelle, whose name I'd picked out of a baby book.

"I'm your mommy," I said to her. "I'm your mommy."

Jacinda changed my life. She forced me to grow up and take control of my decisions. She gave me a reason to wake up each morning. I wanted her to have a better life than I did. I wanted her to feel all the love that I never felt myself.

Her birth also forced the people around me to reassess their assumptions about my life and my decisions. I was a mother now, and a mother is to be respected. The old Sherry who made poor choices was gone; in her place, I was a young woman hoping to make a fresh start.

And my father was quick to notice.

In a sense, Jacinda brought Carl Harris's prodigal daughter home. She and I were a package deal, so if my father wanted to see his lovely granddaughter, he would have to see me too. My family and I had been given a unique opportunity to put the past behind us and start over.

Dad invited Jacinda and me to California as soon as it was safe for her to fly, and when my family picked us up at LAX, they were slack-jawed and rosy at the sight of my button-nose baby with curly black hair. April and Somara couldn't believe they were aunties; they just about fell over each other trying to hold her.

At the house, Dad had converted a spare office into a nursery, crib and all, and from the moment I arrived he and Chris catered to my every need. Dad played with Jacinda every day, and Chris babysat anytime I wanted to spend some quality time with my sisters. At night we sat together for family dinner. After so many years, the Harris clan was whole again.

And the Gore clan seemed to be doing better as well. Darren had been acting less like a bully and more like a father since Jacinda was born; he called every day we were in California to see how she was doing. He also gave me updates on a new job he'd found a few weeks before.

It was big-boy stuff, and I was proud of him for turning over a new leaf. I hoped he could finally emerge from his mother's (considerable) wings and learn to fly; maybe his new job was the type of nudge he needed to leave the nest. I allowed for the possibility that even someone like Darren Gore had the capacity for change.

I think it *is* possible for people to change—no matter who they are. Just look at me. But the change I most hoped for in Darren never came to pass. In fact, things were about to get much worse.

I first knew something was wrong when he called to tell me he was on his way out to Orange County. His reasoning—that he'd accepted a transfer to a new plant in Torrance, California—just didn't add up, and furthermore, we had no money for him to make the trip. I told him on the phone it was a terrible idea, but he wouldn't listen; he said living in Los Angeles was a dream he'd had since childhood. In short, Darren Gore was heading west, and there wasn't much I could do to stop him.

Of course he didn't fly out—that would be the rational choice. As I said earlier, Darren always managed to do the opposite of rational. Instead, he drove the brand-new Volkswagen that we'd bought with the last of our savings—and ran the car into a ditch before he got west of Pensacola. And just when he seemingly couldn't have made a poorer decision, he declined to have the car fixed and instead called AAA to haul him 120 miles west, the maximum distance they allowed. Then he called AAA again and arranged for another tow, for another 120 miles—a process he would repeat again and again, across the *entire United States of America.*

When the AAA tow truck arrived at my dad's house a week later, the driver dumped our smashed Volkswagen off at the curb and Darren hopped out of the cab like he owned the world. My whole family walked out of the house to meet my husband, who hadn't showered in a week. He proceeded to ignore everyone but my father, who was standing on the porch with a pained look on his face.

Darren slapped him on the shoulder.

"You got anything to eat?"

Then he brushed past the rest of us and walked into the house. I felt like crawling into a hole.

Within a few days, my family realized they didn't much like my husband, and it took even less time for me to realize he'd been lying to me for weeks. He confessed he'd been fired from his new job. He'd also ditched our apartment and sold our furniture. It was an epic illustration of personal irresponsibility and illogic, and a perfect example of what he was always doing in our marriage: taking whatever good thing I had going for myself and draining it to the last drop.

We were broke—had been for weeks. But it was okay, he said, because he had a so-called master plan.

"What plan is that?" I asked. I wasn't sure if I really wanted to know.

"Well, it's my dream to live in California, and I figure we can make it out here just as well as anybody else," he said innocently. "So don't worry about it. We'll make the best of things, and with a little help in the short term, we'll be back on our feet in no time."

With a little help . . .

That's when I realized the true nature of Darren's conniving. He wasn't stupid; he knew he was terrible at holding down a job and saving money. So at some point, maybe even as early as our first date, he had dreamed up an idea to con the one person he was supposed to love and cherish most, in order to mooch off the only rich person he knew: my father.

Darren was right. He did have a master plan.

Of course, my father, who could get along with anybody, couldn't stand the sight of Darren. But Darren *was* Jacinda's father, and so my dad did what fathers have done with in-laws for hundreds of years: he tried his best to make it work. Even though Darren went out of his way to exploit his kindness.

When Dad gave us a MasterCard to use for gas, Darren drove everywhere the longest way possible, saying, "The gas is free! May as well live it up!" And when my father asked Darren to keep the house clean, Darren blithely tossed an empty oil can in the driveway.

"Hey, Darren," Dad asked after arriving home from work, "did you by chance throw an empty oil can out front?"

"No."

"Right by your car? In the driveway?"

Darren shook his head.

"Well, do you know who did?"

He sighed. "I said no, Dad."

But Carl Harris wasn't going to leave it at that. He interrogated Darren until he got the truth. And when he did, Dad asked Darren to please not do it again.

Then, just two days later—*two days*—Dad came home and found an empty steering fluid can tossed in the street. He didn't blow up right on the spot, but that night he told me exactly what he thought of my husband, using words I had never heard my father say in his life. Darren really could bring out the worst in anybody.

Perhaps inevitably, our California visit didn't last long. Dad had been looking to relocate to Florida for some time, mostly to be closer to family, and right after Darren arrived, my father found a beautiful property on Tierra Verde Island that he swooped in and bought in a matter of days. Furthermore, Dad told me discretely that Darren wasn't welcome in his new home.

When I told Darren my parents were moving he was crushed; it was obvious we couldn't stay in California without my father's help. Darren had come out to California to chase big dreams, not to go back to the same minimum wage jobs he'd shuffled into and out of all his life. He thought, like a lot of people do, he could be "discovered" in Los Angeles; that fame and fortune and respect would simply show up at his front door. Now that dream was dead, and he was left being normal ol' Darren Gore again. Of course he blamed me for all of it.

Those last few days in California were some of the most terrifying of my life. Bit by bit I watched Darren grow darker, his mood turning malevolent. He would lunge at me and yell—only when we were alone, of course—or threaten to take Jacinda away from me.

The worst of it happened the night Dad took the rest of my

family out of town for a short vacation. During an argument, Darren suddenly flew into a rage and chased me through the house. I escaped into an upstairs bedroom, holding the knob shut so hard my knuckles turned white.

For a moment it was quiet.

Then I heard a sound. What was that? A soft whimper.

I panicked when I knew. *He's got Jacinda.*

He punched at the door so hard the hinges rattled, and I yelled, "Okay! I'll open the door. Just promise to give her to me and I'll open the door."

He didn't answer, so I took a deep breath and undid the bolt. But before I could open the door, he smashed his way in and fell to the ground at my feet — with Jacinda tucked in his arms like a football.

I pulled Jacinda away from him, fled to the downstairs bathroom, and locked the door behind us. We slept in the bathtub that night. Darren banged on the door for hours, shouting, "Wake up! Wake up, baby! If your mommy can't sleep, neither can you!"

I knew right then that my life with Darren was over. That our marriage was over. That I could never again care for this man who could punch through a door holding our daughter like a weapon he might use against me.

He screamed all night; by morning, I was planning my escape from our life together. I didn't believe I could do it right away, however; I was afraid of Darren. I was afraid of what he could do to me, to Jacinda, to my family. So I decided to wait until we were safely back in Florida to tell him I was leaving.

Our Volkswagen was too banged up to make the trip back, and Dad was kind enough to let us drive his Ford Bronco. He even gave us a credit card to cover our travel expenses. Of course, Darren used the card to order the most expensive item at every restaurant along our route.

The drive was terribly long—three thousand miles, four days in all—and my husband and I said very little to each other. I didn't feel well. My head was ringing. At first I thought it might be the heat, but after I got sick in a few gas station restrooms, I began to suspect something else. I'd felt like this before.

Our arduous drive ended at Darren's parents' house. The minute we finished unpacking the car, I excused myself under the guise of running a few errands and drove directly to a drug store, where I bought a home pregnancy test.

Minutes later I read the results: two pink lines. I sat on the toilet and cried hot, desperate tears. Another baby. *Children* instead of *child*. I wondered if I could even do it alone. Did I have the stock to be a single mother of two?

It was a tricky situation. Darren's mind had become feral. His complete lack of empathy frightened me. At that point I believed he was capable of anything. So I chose prudence. I chose to be shrewd. I would bide my time and outthink my husband; I would extricate myself from him with the cunning of a mother forced to protect her flock.

But first I needed to make some money. Fortunately, my father, who had started a new business out of his Florida home, needed plenty of help, and Chris was kind enough to ferry Jacinda and me back and forth. It was a perfect job because it allowed me to tell Darren I needed to work late or stay overnight or spend the weekend at my father's house—and he never realized that I was just trying to stay away from him.

It's not as if he cared anyway. Darren was thrilled that I had a job because it meant he could lie around all day and watch television. He must've assumed I was finally coming around, that I'd finally accepted my fate as a person he could control, because he enthusiastically supported every small change I made around the house and never once questioned my reasons for doing so.

The apartment lease was already in my name, and in the

(stated) interest of simplicity, I changed the other bills into my name too.

Darren was pleased, saying, "I'm glad you're finally learning some responsibility around here."

My final play came on a Sunday, when I placed in front of Darren the myriad of phone messages I'd been collecting for weeks—messages from people looking for him, people to whom he owed money or whose car he'd hit in a parking lot or who accused him of stealing tools from work. There was an entire army of individuals upset with my husband.

I told Darren his financial delinquency was something I would not put up with, and that he would either need to go out and get a job and settle his debts—or get out of the house. Of course, I knew he would flat out refuse, and when he did, I surprised him by saying, "Okay, well, then this is goodbye."

Then I walked out the front door with Jacinda in my arms.

Only then, after we were long gone, did Darren realize that our apartment lease, which was in my name, hadn't been renewed for another month; that our phone had been cancelled; that my clothes were no longer in the house, nor were Jacinda's crib, toys, or diapers; or that there wasn't a morsel of food in the cupboards.

I had escaped Darren Gore, and I had done it in plain sight.

On March 18, one year to the day after Jacinda's birth, and two years to the day after my wedding, I delivered Shannon Summer Marie Gore. I gave her my sisters' two middle names—April Shannon and Somara Summer—along with the name Marie, which is my middle name and a Harris family tradition.

Shannon was delicate and small, with the purest, whitest hair one could imagine, and when she first cried, it was as soft as a kitten's purr. I took her home to a two-bedroom apartment I rented across from my father's house. Darren didn't ask for custody during the divorce, which was quick and painless. He knew what he was and what he'd done.

More than anything, I think he was surprised. It probably never occurred to him that I could actually leave.

Or that the con artist could so easily be outsmarted.

Chapter 9

TOBY

I was now a single mother of two.

I'd extricated myself from a bad situation with an emotionally abusive husband while protecting my girls, and I'd planned enough in advance to make sure we could live a stable life after my divorce.

Still, it was disconcerting. In the past, I had always been the one who'd made the mistakes, but this time I felt as if I'd done all the right things, and yet here I was again—starting over and trying to rebuild my life.

But this time *was* different in one way: I was happy.

Only a few years earlier I'd been wasting away in a terrible depression, unable to find any reason to continue. Now I had two beautiful little baby girls who desperately needed me to make things right. Their love gave me strength I hadn't had before. They kept me focused on the tasks at hand. I knew that if I didn't figure out what to do, it would be Jacinda and Shannon who would suffer. And I would not have that at all.

The girls would get a better life than I got—that was my promise to myself. And not in terms of money or toys or cars or houses. I knew I might never achieve those things. But I could most certainly give them all the love they needed, all the love I'd so often desired myself.

So together we struggled, and we survived.

I continued to work for my father, who was in the midst of his own late-in-life, personal resurgence on Tierra Verde Island.

The pressures of Orange County had worn him down over the years, but returning home to Florida had lightened him up again. He became more like he used to be when he was young—laid-back and easygoing. He jet-skied. He threw parties.

On Sundays he often invited friends and family over to barbeque on the water, and it was at one of those large parties that I happened to meet somebody new, somebody that would play a large part in the rest of my life.

When I first saw him, I was sipping iced tea next to the pool.

"Hey, Sherry! Congrats on the little girls!" said my friend Michelle, pulling up a chair. "I bet they're a handful."

"Michelle, you have no idea."

I took another sip.

"Boy, I'd like to get my hands on that head of hair."

"Sorry?"

I thought she was talking about my girls, but then I saw she was pointing at a man sitting poolside.

"Him," she said. "I'd like to do his hair." Michelle was a beautician.

I squinted into the sun. It *was* some great hair. Thick, blond, and shoulder-length.

"Who is that?" I asked her.

His name was Toby, I found out later, and he was into heavy metal—a rocker. He was a guy's guy, and he'd recently befriended my father.

Toby and I didn't speak much during that first afternoon at Dad's house, but in the ensuing weeks we became friendly. Each time we ran in to each other, he never failed to compliment me on how I looked or inquire about the children or even play with them if they were around. He was the first guy I'd met since the girls were born that didn't seem scared of them.

Then one night I ran into Toby at a restaurant. I happened

to be on a disastrous blind date, and so Toby and I didn't have much of a chance to speak. But he called me later that evening.

"How come you're home already?" he said when I answered. "It's not even eleven."

"Don't."

"Don't what?" He could barely contain a giggle. "Your date looked like one real cool dude."

"Now you're being sarcastic."

"So you're saying it wasn't a love connection?"

"I'd never tell you."

"Well, he better have at least treated you well."

"Yeah? Why's that?"

"You deserve it."

I laughed him off. "Don't be jealous, Toby."

"I'm not jealous."

"You are, even though you know that guy was a total creep."

"Maybe during dates it's you who acts like a creep."

"You'll never know."

"We'll see."

"Who? Who will see?"

"Well ..." He went silent for a bit. "Maybe us. Sometime."

This was new. I fiddled for words.

"What do you think?" he said finally.

"Toby, are you asking me out?"

"Only if you say yes. If you say no, then I will deny it forever."

"Okay. Okay." I pretended to mull it over. "Sure. Yes. *Maybe* I'll go on one date with you—but only so you can find out."

"Find what out?"

"Whether I'm a creep or not."

"Okay. Next Saturday then. Your house."

I smiled to myself. "It's a date. See you then."

The following Saturday, Toby drove down to St. Petersburg

from New Port Richey, a small town about an hour north. I couldn't get a sitter for the girls, so Toby and I eschewed a traditional date night to hang around the house instead. He was cautious around the girls, but kind, and I could tell he enjoyed them. We had a delightful meal together, and then, later on in the evening, when it was time for him to leave, he promised to visit again the next weekend. And he did. And he came over the weekend after that.

In the beginning, we kept our relationship slow and very cautious. I was still deeply hurt by what happened with Darren, and I wasn't sure if I could ever open my heart to another man. I was also dead serious about the health of my children. There was no way I was going to hop right into another serious relationship without knowing—for sure this time—whether the guy would turn into a pumpkin right after midnight.

But I couldn't ignore my feelings for Toby, nor the way he respected my children. I began to look forward all week to our weekends together—little pockets of domestic bliss spent watching television, playing games with the children, and eating home-cooked meals.

And then one night, after he'd helped me put the children to bed, Toby turned to me on the couch and said, "Sherry, I love you."

My heart nearly leapt out of my throat.

He continued, "I can't believe I'm saying this—but I also really care for your girls. It's not like I grew up wanting children. Truth is—I've never even thought of it before. But these afternoons when I come over, when we're all together ... it just makes me feel like I've been missing something my whole life, and I just recently realized what it is."

"What?"

"Family, Sherry. A family."

Those were the same words Darren had once said to me, and I'd married him because of them. Could I trust again?

The light of the television blinked across Toby's sturdy face; silhouette figures dancing in red, green, and yellow.

"You don't have to say anything now," he said. "I just want you to know that I care. And if you're not ready for a serious relationship, then I'll wait." He took my hand. "You hear me, Sherry? I will wait."

Those words would prove to be true, but not in any way that Toby and I could've imagined right then.

He and I continued our same schedule—together on the weekends, apart during the week—for quite a while longer before I decided to move in with him. I said yes because I loved him, and because I knew he could be the father the girls didn't have, the father Darren Gore could never become.

It was the second time I'd moved in with a man before marriage, and I knew even then that it wasn't what God instructs us to do. But though I'd enjoyed church in Escondido, and though I'd enjoyed it when Cousin Judy read Bible stories to her children, I wasn't committed to the Christian faith, and I didn't know God's full perspective on life and marriage.

I only knew that Toby was a good man and that he was good to my children. And being the responsible woman I was attempting to be, that was enough.

Toby lived in New Port Richey, a port town crowded with strip malls, snakes, alligators, and retirees. He owned a small, ranch-style house with a fenced-in yard dotted with oak trees. The house was a bit smaller than my apartment, but we felt snug rather than cramped, and it became "home" the moment we put down our belongings. The walls seemed to close around us like a big tent, protective and serene. Our universe was that little house.

Toby worked six days a week at UPS, and when he wasn't at work, he dutifully helped out around the house. When it was time for Jacinda to take a bath, he liked to stick her out in the front yard, yell, "Catch the water!" and spray her down with the garden hose.

They were good times. I got a part-time job at a tanning salon, which was Toby's idea. He wanted me to have a social life outside of him and the children. He wanted me to be happy. He listened in awe when I told him stories of my disc jockey days, and he encouraged me to go back to school once Shannon was old enough, to continue my media career.

Soon he asked me to marry him, and he did it in a way that was as simple and as easy as he was. He merely looked up and said, "Hey, this is working, right? So do you think we should get married?"

I said of course I did.

We busied ourselves planning a simple ceremony, and in the midst of our preparations, I got another unexpected gift. I was going to have another baby. I was speechless. Previously I had to worry about bringing a little baby into a world dominated by an abusive husband. But this time I would share one of life's greatest joys—having a child—with a man who was up to the challenge.

I did worry about telling him, though. Toby was an emotional guy, and I didn't know how he would react at first. So I decided to say it simply, just like he had done when he asked me to be his wife. I cooked him a nice dinner, and then, while he was stuffing himself with button mushrooms and lobster tails, I told him he was going to be a father.

He didn't say anything at first; in fact, the only sound came from the fork he dropped onto his plate. Then he slowly pushed away from the table, stood up, and walked into our bedroom. I knew him well enough to let him fall asleep before I came in.

Toby dealt with things in his own way—I knew that—but I didn't expect him to avoid me for the next three days. He'd been nothing but a good man to me, so I didn't doubt that he would come around, but still—I was nervous. What if, somehow, he wasn't ready? Had I overestimated him? Was I making the same mistake that I'd made with my former husband?

I kept repeating the same thing over and over in my head: *He'll get there. He'll come through.*

Then, on the fourth day, he walked into the kitchen just as I was finishing my breakfast, kissed me on the cheek, whispered, "I can't wait," and broke into the biggest, brightest smile I'd ever seen him make.

We were married a few months later in front of seventy friends and family. The ceremony was in our backyard—an oasis of majestic oaks and blooming azaleas. I wore a beautiful crème dress—no bikini this time—and Toby filled out a sharp suit. My father walked me down the aisle. April and Somara were bridesmaids. Even my mother showed. It was a dream come true.

The dream didn't stop there either, for only a month later, Toby and I went to the doctor for an ultrasound and learned we were going to have a little boy.

The news made me so happy, but Toby was curiously quiet, and when we got home, he went into our bedroom and shut the door behind him. I walked in and sat on the bed. He was crying.

"Hey—don't cry, honey," I said. "What's wrong? Are you sad it's a boy?"

"No, I'm not sad," he said, sobbing gently. "It's just that, once he's born, nobody is ever going to understand that I love the girls just as much as if they were mine too. I can't love him more than I love them—I can't—and I just wish I could let everybody know that. Other people won't understand, but it's true. It will always be true."

Tyler was born five months later, the epitome of a bouncing

baby boy, as wild as a tempest and twice as loud. Toby took to him all-heart and all-love with an intensity that never wavered, and yet he never let that intensity drown out the love he'd already banked with my two girls.

For Toby was a good man, and he always will be.

Chapter 10

THE DEEPEST HOLE

Years before I met Toby, when I was twenty years old, Dad, April and I sat on the couch watching *Webster.* It was a "very special" episode, the kind that showed characters facing a serious problem, as in: "This week on *The Facts of Life,* a very special episode where Blair deals with divorce." In the '80s, these sorts of episodes aired frequently, offering a thin slice of melodrama before wrapping up neatly in less than a half hour.

It was maudlin stuff, but this particular *Webster* episode was something different, for its "issue," child molestation, had occurred to someone in our own family—April.

Her abuse had occurred years earlier, at the hands of a babysitter's "helper," and when my dad found out about it, he had chosen to keep quiet instead of pressing charges. Back then, where we lived, it was considered taboo to splash a tawdry story all over the papers; rather, families swept dark secrets under the rug. So Dad never told the police what happened. He never confronted the teenager.

But I knew about it. And as I watched that *Webster* episode I grappled with my own guilt. I felt it was wrong to cover up a crime. For one, the guilty go free. And two, it sends a specific message to the victim: "Your pain is a cross that you will bear alone."

Of course on television, where writers can turn a complex

reality into a simple solution, Webster made the right decision, and the episode ended on a positive note. I didn't think my family's real-world version had done the same, and suddenly I found I could not hold my tongue any longer.

I turned to April. "You know if anyone ever does anything like that to you ever again you don't have to keep it a secret."

"Sherry!" my dad hissed. "Be quiet!"

"Dad, she—"

"We are not going to talk about this!" He pointed at my sister. "April, go to your room right now."

She hopped off the couch and disappeared; my father turned off the television and glared at me, his anger thickening the air in the room. I held his gaze. It was an intense moment, which is probably why neither one of us heard April creep back in and crawl behind the sofa.

I suddenly blurted out, "You should let April talk about what happened to her."

"You don't understand." His voice was ice cold.

"But she'll have to deal with it someday."

"She might not even remember it, Sherry. Be quiet."

"But Dad you can't just . . ."

"Sherry!" he roared, red as a plum. "Shut your mouth! You leave her alone so she can forget!"

The violence in his voice propelled me to my feet, as if I had to combat his emotion with my fists.

"She won't forget!"

"How can you know that?"

"Because *I* remember!" It was true. I did remember. A similar thing had happened to me when I was very young.

He was shocked that I brought it up. His face softened, and I could see he was sorry for failing to protect us. But that's not what I was angry about—a parent can't be everywhere. I was upset because he had kept quiet. I was upset because for years I'd supposed that what happened to me was my own fault. Because for years I'd considered myself used garbage.

I refused to let April feel that way.

In a low voice, I asked, "Why didn't you do anything afterward?"

I could tell he wasn't prepared to answer the question, not after all this time. His eyes drifted past the walls of our living room to somewhere beyond physical space, to the place where we hide memories that don't make any sense.

When he spoke again he was like a child in trouble with his mother.

"I made sure that boy never stepped foot on our property again."

He shook his head and folded his arms. For a brief moment, I thought he might finally breach the wall we'd built between ourselves, take me in his arms, and tell me everything was okay. I could see the possibility flicker over his face.

Then it was gone, just as quickly as it had appeared.

"You hear me now, Sherry," he said slowly. "If you ever tell anyone what happened to your sister I will disown you. You will never be allowed in this house again. If I see you in public, I will pretend I don't know you. And you will never, *ever* see either one of your sisters again for the rest of your life."

He pointed at me. "You hear?"

"Yes."

It wouldn't be until 2003 that I would learn April had been in the room, that she'd heard our entire conversation. She and I were adults by the time she told me. She said that in her darkest days, she'd drawn strength from the way I'd stood up for her. The argument I had with our father became a bond between us—one that lasted years. I promised I would always protect her. And I did protect her. Right up until the day when I couldn't.

But long before that, long before the awful morning at April's apartment when I realized she was gone, we were forced to grieve together. It was Mother's Day 1996. I was having lunch in the backyard with my family, Somara, and our neighbor Maria and her family when we got the call. Toby answered.

"Your Dad has been in a diving accident," he told me, placing the phone back on the hook. "Get your things. We need to go to St. Petersburg right now." I knew by his tone that my father was already dead.

Toby said little on the drive from New Port Richey to St. Petersburg. I think he kept silent on purpose. I'm sure he wanted to give me ninety minutes of calm before the hammer dropped, much in the same way that I, years later, would wish April's boys could take forever leaving that dreadful apartment. Because when death happens, nobody is the same after. The hard part is figuring out how you're going to change.

Toby and I drove to my parents' house where everyone had gathered. Chris was beside herself, the grief overwhelming. She'd been married to my father for twenty-four years. She was so young; a forty-three-year-old widow. Any latent bitterness I had toward her dissolved the moment I saw her red swollen eyes. I just wanted to take her pain away.

She was with my father when he died. They were diving seven miles off Fort De Soto, near Egmont Key, when Dad suddenly shot to the surface, tore off his mask, gasped, "I can't breathe!" and sank. Mikey, Dad's diving partner, found him under the surface and hauled his limp body to the boat. Chris gave him CPR all the way back to shore.

He'd had a massive heart attack, and died instantly.

Chris arranged for services at the David C. Gross Funeral Home in St. Petersburg. The day before the ceremony, my family visited the funeral home for a final look at Dad before he was cremated. I remember an attendant walking us down a long hallway, and each step was more dreadful than the last. I'd never seen the body of a person I loved.

We ended up in a small room. I assumed my father would be arranged tastefully, but it was more like a nightmare come true. A cheap purple blanket stained with bleach covered him up to the neck; harsh overhead lights shaded his skin a greenish yellow. I noticed something glistening near his chin; it was a zipper. He was still in the body bag. An intolerable smell burned in my nose.

A man works hard for fifty-three years, and this is how it ends?

The following afternoon we gathered for the funeral. Dad's friends and family from Florida were there, but no one from California showed. Maybe he hadn't had many friends in Orange County. Maybe he'd been such a different person out there that few people got close to him.

Or maybe he wasn't *seen* in California. I guess in death, my father and I had something in common after all.

After the service was over I sat on the funeral home steps and cried to myself. I'd hoped the service would ease the rejection I felt, but if anything, I hurt even more. My father was so much brighter when he returned to Florida. Fun-loving Butch Harris had come back. He'd rekindled so many relationships.

But never with me. I kept waiting for our time to come but it never did. Now I realized it never would.

He would never tell me I meant something to him. He would never say he was sorry for what had happened to April when she was a child.

That's all I really needed—one "I'm sorry." For everything. Then I'd be okay.

But that chance was gone.

A thick black gauze—that is what covered my world after

Dad died. It wasn't normal grief. I felt suspended in time, an old vinyl record skipping in place.

I wondered whether every identity I'd assumed in my life—doting daughter, Belinda Carlisle, Tuesday, disc jockey, wife, mother—was, at some level, created to get my father to see me. To get him to accept that I existed in his world. That I wasn't a flunkie. My life had been defined by that need, but now its object—my father—was gone. Forever. And when he left, he seemed to take my reason to exist right along with him. Once again, I felt like a ghost. I felt like there was a Sherry-sized hole in the universe.

Toby didn't have a clue what to do; I could barely get out of bed and spent hours crying behind closed doors. I quit eating. I would lie next to Tyler's crib, my mind blank, feeling the earth fly around the sun. Toby did what he could to sympathize, but he had the children to deal with and his work. He couldn't stay home all day just because his wife was spiraling into an existential pit.

But there was someone in our lives who could. Her name was Maria. And soon her kindness would set me on a path to rebirth.

Maria lived with her family in the house behind ours. She and I were already good friends before the tragedy, but after the funeral, we became much closer. She stopped by whenever I needed someone to talk to, and we often spoke about my struggles or my father. Sometimes I would just ask Maria to tell me stories from her own life. She wove beautiful tales about her children and her upbringing, her life and her faith. I felt at peace listening to her talk.

Maria was a devout Christian, and when she spoke about Jesus I felt the strength of her words. Her whole world revolved around her faith, and her faith gave her a sense of assurance I'd never experienced myself. Maria knew she was loved by God.

I, on the other hand, had spent most of my life wondering if anyone could love me at all.

I wanted to feel that love, but when Maria first asked me if I wished to attend church with her, I said no. I didn't think I deserved it. I thought I was a lost cause. I said no again and again—and she just kept right on asking. Finally I said yes just to get her to stop.

I was still fearful the day we attended First Baptist Church of Jasmine Lakes. I almost walked out during the first hymn, not because I disliked the service or congregation, but quite the opposite: I felt ashamed. Like I was an interloper, a spy. Such blackness had covered my heart that I felt too dirty to be accepted by God. It was too late for me, I thought.

But then the pastor stood up for his sermon, and what came next turned my entire world upside down.

"Some of you in this room have made mistakes in life," he said. "Some of you have faced situations others cannot imagine, and you still shudder under the ramifications, year after year.

"But you do not recognize the source of your pain. Your actions—your decisions—whether made on account of hate, spite, envy, or regret, cannot be judged by man. Man cannot listen to you fully, nor can he understand your need. There is only one who can. And it is He who you must seek to find relief."

Relief?

"Yes, relief."

Was he talking to me?

"From yourself, from your past, from your demons, and from the dark hand of those who would lead you astray. But you cannot be led astray if you are part of the flock, and so I ask each of you, I implore each of you: Forget those people who've imprisoned you with neglect or need. Forget those you must please. Instead, look to the Shepherd, who gave His life for your sins and who wishes to give you life again after death."

Pinpricks dotted my shoulders. The people sitting around me slowly faded from sight.

"Many of you have gone through this life feeling unloved."

I had.

"You may have been told you are worthless."

I looked at my hands and they were covered in tears. *Whose hands are these?* I wondered. *Whose eyes?*

"You may have even felt that a special place in hell was reserved for the likes of you."

I had been told this by my own heart.

"But let me say now that it is a lie." His voice pitched to the ceiling. "And I stand before you to declare that Christ died for your sins. All of them." He cast his eyes at his flock. "All of them."

He cast his eyes at me. *"All of them!"*

The pastor was speaking, but behind his words, I heard something more. Someone more.

"And where is He, the one with the power to give you new life? He is in this room. Right now. And He loves you."

At "you," I leaned forward and my legs lost their gravity. I slid against the wooden pew in front of me, then down to the floor, to my knees—Maria's warm hand on my back.

What was happening to me?

"You are His child. Don't you see what this means? He is God, creator of the entire universe—and yet His only wish is for your salvation."

The room grew dim ... were the lights flickering? No, but my view was no longer of the church or the pulpit. Instead I could only see light—beaming from the pastor straight to me, in a sharp tunnel. I was inside a golden sphere. I took two handfuls of beige carpet to steady myself and rested my head on my chest. It was too bright to look at the pastor. With my eyes closed, his words lit up my mind.

"You don't have to live with your pain any longer."

Golden words.

"There is one who has already paid your price for you."

I hoped he was right.

"He only waits for you to realize what He has paid."

Could it be that simple?

"And for you to love Him."

Against the black of my eyelids, I saw a road.

"Won't you?"

The road led away from my body and away from the congregation, up to the pastor and through him, to the horizon just behind ...

"Can you do what He asks?"

... the road bent with the curve of the earth, circumnavigating the globe, until it arrived at the front of the church again, where I'd walked in only minutes before. In my mind I turned, and the road pushed into me, where it stopped at the center of my fleshy heart.

"Won't you love Him?"

A heart that suddenly beat for the first time, like a baby's, warm and new.

"Won't you love Him today?"

As the pastor spoke, I knew my old life—my many lives—was passing away, shed from my body like an outer skin. I felt weightless—free. Free like I had never felt before.

"Will you love Him?"

Opening my eyes, I saw that Pastor Francis stood over me. I was in the front of the church, alone and crying.

"Are you looking for forgiveness today?"

"I am."

He knelt next to me, two little houses in the sky.

"Then let us pray."

As he spoke I heard the trumpets, the sheer *lyricism* of the universe, instead of his voice. And amidst that roaring melody, I prayed: "I am so sorry, God. For everything. Can You know that? Look here in my chest and please see that I am. For craving and for desiring. For my choices. For a marriage I could not hold, for the father I blamed, and for what I've done to myself. But most of all, please forgive me for hearing You all my life but never listening. Somehow You have brought me here. And I don't want to live another day if I have to live as I have in the past. Just let me die," I prayed, "or let me in."

I don't remember the pastor finishing his prayer, helping me up, or ushering me back to my seat. I don't remember the crazy looks people must have given me, or what Maria said when I sat back down. I don't remember the end of the service or the car ride home or my children or Toby.

But I do remember that around six o'clock that same night, September 26, 1996, I slipped out after dinner wearing a dress and carrying a pair of jeans and a white T-shirt rolled up in a bath towel. I remember driving back to the church and going inside, speaking with a few strangers, and then climbing into three feet of water. And I remember feeling clean when I climbed out.

In that water I made a choice. A plain choice. A choice for God.

Chapter 11

My Name Was Sherry

When Pastor Francis put me in the water it was glorious. I felt I was claiming a mantle created and carefully previsualized at the beginning of time. God had waited for me for thousands upon thousands of years. And here I was, finally, dripping wet on His doorstep.

I was baptized in front of strangers, an appropriate beginning, for much of what I would do over the next four years would place me among unfamiliar faces. But long before I looked out into those faces, I first had to look into Toby's, and when I got home from the church and told him I'd been baptized, I could tell by his face that I'd hurt his feelings.

"And you didn't ask me to come?"

"No, Toby. I didn't."

"But why?"

"I don't know. It's just something I had to do by myself."

"But I'm your husband, Sherry," he said. "I could've supported you."

"I know, Tobin." I called him Tobin when I felt sorry. "But I didn't need support tonight. I needed to do this myself."

We said little to each other for the rest of the evening. I wish I'd known then how to make my feelings clear—maybe I could've spared us some of the pain to come. But I didn't. I could hardly understand what had happened.

I lay awake in bed for most of the night thinking about my baptism. I was afraid to sleep. I was afraid that somehow the baptism wouldn't take, that I'd wake up in the morning the same old Sherry Gore again. As my eyelids grew heavier I tried reading a book but found I couldn't follow the words. I turned on the television, but the sound warbled in my head and I couldn't make sense of it. I was distracted by things beyond me, things calling out for my attention.

Finally, I drifted off to sleep, and that night my dreams were terrifying. I lived and relived days from my past in a nightmare state. Tuesday on the beach. Darren chasing me into the bathroom. My father's face in that body bag.

Looking back now on that night of a thousand years, I see that those dreams were appropriate, because I *was* reliving those moments, those emotions, every day of my waking life—and had been for thirty-one years. I like to think those dreams were a way for me to remember all those pre-Christian days, to take them out for a final spin—right there at the end. Because I had been on a carousel my whole life, and now, I was about to get off.

When I opened my eyes the next morning, my first thought was to thank God I'd made it through. I looked at the ceiling.

Something was different.

I rolled over and placed my hand on my chest. Where was the heart I'd had before? The one blackened with resentment? That previous heart had ached, but this one ... I could *feel* the blood in my arms; it rushed like wildflower seeds chuting down a gust of wind. I imagined red cells carrying strength and light through bio-tunnels of living flesh. I sat up in bed and balled my fists in front of my face.

It felt like I could punch through the universe to the other side.

My bedroom seemed the same—four walls, one ceiling, one floor—but now none of it seemed real. More like a dream ... Dorothy's Technicolor Oz.

I was thirty-one years old. My name was Sherry. I'd been married twice and had three children. And in September 1996, I was seeing, for the first time, the world as God intends.

In the bathroom I splashed some water on my face, and when I looked into the mirror, I saw my father staring back at me. We both smiled together, and suddenly, without notice, I found I could forgive him for everything. All the regret and resentment fell from both our faces and plopped down into the sink. The faucet washed them away.

Our burden was over, because while I'd previously had one father, now I had two. And the second one was perfect so the first one wouldn't have to be.

I put on a robe and walked out into the living room, where the smell of bacon tickled my nose. Toby was in the kitchen. I'd hurt his feelings the night before, and he'd responded by making breakfast.

I wondered, "Is it even possible to tell him how I feel right now?"

I couldn't fathom what words I could use. It would be like a person explaining the northern lights.

After breakfast, an idea popped into my head, so I excused myself from the table and drifted back to the bedroom, where I found a footstool and placed it in my closet. Then I climbed up onto the stool and reached as far back into the deep recesses of our closet shelf as I could.

In high school, I remembered learning that light from the beginning of the universe takes so long to travel to the earth that astronomers looking into that light can see the universe in its earliest days of creation; well, a bedroom closet is like that too—for the deeper one looks, the further back in time one is able to see.

First, I found trinkets from my first days with Toby. Further in, I spotted a picture from my hotdog-stand wedding, my journal from California, and a radio license from my time as a disc jockey. And near the very back of the closet, I even brushed past a picture of my green dune buggy convertible, a bleach-blond sixteen-year-old standing near the hood. I vaguely recognized her as me.

And then I found what I was looking for, against the closet wall: a relic of my fourteenth year, still as bright and as clean as the day it was given to me.

It was a Bible, white and leather-bound, with my name embossed in gold. A gift from my godparents. Back then it had been a disappointing gift, but now I saw the true nature of God's Plan — for seventeen years later, I needed that book more than life itself.

I took the Bible into the living room and snuggled up on the couch with Tyler in my arms. I looked into his tiny face.

"You, my little sweet son," I thought to myself, "are going to be spared a painful life."

I was wrong in thinking that becoming a Christian meant our lives would no longer be difficult. There would be painful times ahead; I would make decisions that no parent should have to face. But I didn't need to know about all that right then, as I stared into my son's innocent eyes. All I needed to know was that I would never again face an uncertain future alone. God was now at my side.

He had given me a clean slate after a lifetime of mistakes, and I made a vow to Him, right then and there, to do whatever He asked of me.

It wasn't the first vow I'd made, but it would become the one vow I would keep.

That first day I awoke a Christian came and went as none had before — a dizzying fantasy as thrilling and mysterious as young love.

God had given me new life, and as a mother, I understood that with new life comes confusion. I was curious and
unformed—like a child. Raw data rocketed over me in waves.
Sensate emotions burst forth that I couldn't grasp. In a search
for understanding, I read the Bible four or five hours a day,
poring over difficult passages with a rigor I'd never approached
in school.

And just as a child learns the most in the earliest days, I learned
much in those first few months reading the Bible, some of which
gave me reason to consider making subtle changes to my life.
Now, I have to stress that these changes did not happen quickly,
nor with ease. Much of what I did took *years* to accomplish, and
with each change came plenty of strange looks and caustic asides.
But I was determined to keep the vow I made before God.

The first change I made was to become a member of a Baptist
church close to our home. I chose the church over Maria's
because it was a smaller, more conservative congregation, and
because it had an excellent school I was excited to have the girls
attend. Toby supported my decision to choose private school
over public, and any lingering concerns he may have had disappeared as we watched Jacinda and Shannon thrive in a more
wholesome teaching environment.

I changed things around our home too; though, as I said, it
was a long process. I was first moved to change the contents of
my wardrobe because of a passage I read in Timothy:

Women should adorn themselves in respectable apparel,
with modesty and self-control, not with braided hair and gold
or pearls or costly attire, but with what is proper for women
who profess godliness — with good works.

(1 Timothy 2:9 – 10 ESV)

When I looked at the short skirts and low-cut tops littering my bedroom closet, I shuddered. They were designed to

configure the body, to conceal flaws, to draw attention. Before, I'd loved putting myself into those fabrics. But now they seemed fake. So I threw them out and filled my wardrobe with ankle-length dresses I purchased at thrift stores instead.

I also read a passage in the Old Testament that asked women to let their hair grow long and natural, so I stopped cutting mine and threw out the chemical bleach keeping me blond since I was sixteen. Then I put the straightening iron under the sink, finally letting my naturally kinky, curly hair grow free.

Again, Toby stood by all of these decisions. He cherished the new, positive spirit now animating my life. He even told me that I looked just as beautiful to him in a modest dress as I had in a skirt and high heels—a crucial show of support that not all men would have made.

Many of my friends, on the other hand—some of them religious, some not—reacted with an uneasy fatigue. They cautioned me to slow down, to act normal. To go to church on Sundays like everybody else, and let that be enough.

I remember one instance in particular when a fellow parent from the girls' school stopped me in the parking lot before church.

"Oh dear," he said. "Sherry, you don't look well today. Are you feeling sick?"

"I feel fine."

"Oh, but you're so pale. You might be coming down with something."

I brushed at the front of my dress. "Well, I don't know what to say. I feel good." Then I remembered. "Oh! Maybe it's because I'm not wearing any makeup!"

He chuckled. "I see. Got up a little late for church today?"

"Um . . . no . . . we were on time . . ."

"So you just didn't wear any?"

"Yes, that's right."

We stood awkwardly for a moment, and I felt I owed him some clarification.

So I said, "I read in the book of Esther that she turned down the cosmetics she was offered to make her more beautiful. She wanted to present herself to the king as she was." I smiled. "I just wanted to do the same for God."

"Ah," he said, "you know your Bible, Sherry. It does say that. But you know . . . we don't always have to take everything in the Bible as a commandment. The Old Testament was written long ago, and so we adapt our understanding of its meaning through the years."

He cupped his hand over his mouth. "You know what my wife says? 'If the barn needs painting—paint it!'"

That short conversation was a pivotal moment in my Christian life, because it's when I first realized that people live their faith, and their interpretation of God's Word, in many different ways.

Since then, I've learned that the decisions we make as Christians reflect how God speaks to each one of us in our heart. It's not our place to tell other people what to do or to judge. It is only our place to listen. God's house is easily big enough for me and my plain dresses and women who dress fashionably. For "unpainted" and "painted" faces. Our responsibility is to find out which path God is calling us to walk—and to walk it with humility.

My path serviced a strict interpretation of the Bible because I was weak, like a child. I needed time to grow. So I could never be a Sunday-only church gal. I had to be all in; I needed God next to me at all times to keep me from sliding back into despair.

And once I made my investment in Christ, I witnessed miraculous changes in both myself and my home. God's love uncorked a confidence inside of me that I'd never had. Suddenly, I felt wanted. I felt *seen*. And with the change in my own disposition, the dark clouds lifted from our house. We played more games together. We laughed all the time. The children took pleasure in the newly ordered state of things, and they were happier people as a result. In time, they grew as excited about their own faith as I was about mine, and we bonded every night over stories about Jonah and the whale, Noah's ark, and the twelve disciples.

Years ago, I'd walked into my cousin Judy's house a homeless teen and experienced this same wholesome family dynamic. Now I had managed to recreate it in my own home with the people I loved.

It took me a long time to find out who I really was inside, and after God gave me my first peek, I did everything I could to grow into the person He wanted me to become. Already the changes I'd made were startling: I'd catch sight of myself in a rearview mirror—curly natural hair, simple dress, gaggle of kids in the backseat—and couldn't believe it was the same girl who'd slept on the beach under a lifeguard stand.

I never wanted to go back there. To the way I used to feel. And as months, even years, fell away, and I spent more time with my Bible, more time attempting to follow its lead, I made more and more changes to my house and home.

I first decided to wear a head covering in response to 1 Corinthians 11, which states:

> But every woman who prays or prophesies with her head uncovered dishonors her head—it is the same as having her head shaved.

For me, without judgment toward others, wearing a head covering illustrated my commitment to God. It also served as a helpful reminder: each time I placed a covering on my head, I was reminded about my vow to Christ, my responsibility for living His Plan.

Responsibility—that's a key word in the slow transformation I was engaged in, because I had my children's spiritual well-being to think about as well. I wanted to carve out a set of godly values they could use for the rest of their lives, and the more I looked around our house, the more things I objected to.

Television is a good example. There were programs we loved—PBS was always a favorite in our house—but surrounding those programs were commercials and distractions unfit for the way I wanted us to live. So after a long period of consideration, I threw out the TV. My children never seemed to miss it. I remember our local librarian asking Shannon one time, "If you don't watch TV, what do you do for fun?"

Shannon answered, "We're too busy having our own adventures to sit inside and watch other people have theirs."

Each time I heard something like that come from my children I knew I was on the right track.

I went through their toys too, to make sure none of it was contrary to our Christian values. Anything that ran on batteries or screens or made obnoxious noises was out; Lincoln Logs, building blocks, board games, paper dolls, jump ropes, jacks, paints, paper and crayons were in. And we could never have too many books.

I encouraged the children to play outside rather than indoors and populated our backyard with rabbits and chicks to teach responsibility. We had a blast raising those animals together; the sound of bunnies pushing their food bowls around their cages, or fresh peeps from fifty chicks at sunrise, were all it took to get Jacinda, Shannon, and Tyler hopping from their beds and racing off to take care of their brood.

They were learning how to live healthy lives through responsibility and engagement, and they were learning it as children. I'd only found those things as an adult. And on my own account, there was still much work left to do.

Chapter 12

THE BIGGEST UNADVERTISED RESORT IN THE WORLD

Toby never had an issue with the Christian values I was instilling in our home, the changes I made to myself, the new lessons I was teaching our children, or my new focus on Jesus Christ.

But there were things in our marriage that troubled us both, and as I grew more committed in my faith, we entered a difficult period in our lives together.

He is a private man, and there is not too much I can say about this issue—only that during the first few years after I became a Christian, he and I separated, and that it was a mutual decision, motivated by faith and other factors, that necessitated Toby pay full attention to his own health and well-being.

When it happened, I realized more than ever that I needed a community. There was just too much heartache in this world to stand against it by myself. I loved the people at my church, but as my personal relationship with Christ grew, I began to wonder if there were other churches more suited to my needs. It was just a feeling I had. An intuition—something stronger than gravity pulling at my heart.

I prayed every night that God might help me find people

who could teach me in the same ways I taught my children. I had no idea where to look. And then one day I had the most intriguing thought, something God must've placed firmly in my head:

"What would Carl Harris do?"

My father had taught himself computers. It was how he'd built such a successful career for himself—by taking responsibility for learning what he wanted to know. Wasn't I in a similar situation, in that I wanted to build a career—a career in faithful living?

I knew exactly what my father would do in my place—he'd go to the library. So that's where I went. At the New Port Richey Public Library I asked the librarian where I could find a few books on Christianity. She showed me to the comparative religion section—a daunting mélange of religious tomes, manuscripts, and theoretical treatises—that at first left me feeling quite overwhelmed. It seemed like it would take a lifetime to get through it all.

Fortunately, I had a lifetime to give, so with a shrug and a bit of caffeine, I pulled five or ten books from the shelves, plopped down at a table, and started to read.

I first read about all the Baptist Christian denominations, why they existed, and where they came from. Then I read about the Lutherans, the Methodists, the Seventh-day Adventists, the Jehovah's Witnesses, the Presbyterians, the Pentecostals, the nondenominationals, and even the Mormons. Each branch of the Christian faith had its own origin story, its own heroes and villains, and its own raison d'être—colorful histories rich in mystery and adventure.

I also read about how Martin Luther and his followers split Christianity into Catholicism and Protestantism, and as I traced a line from past to present, I stumbled upon stories of the Anabaptists, whom I already knew about and respected. These were people who put their doctrine and their belief in God above all else—and who were often martyred because of it. They were always fleeing, always starting over someplace else.

It's no wonder that I identified with them from the start.

I did learn something new, however, when I read about an early Anabaptist named Menno Simons, who focused communities into small bands of God-fearing people living apart from the modern world. They were called Mennonites, in his name. Then I read about a Mennonite, Jakob Ammann, living a hundred years after Menno's death, who carved out an even smaller population of people who were steadfast in their refusal to conform to contemporary culture. They too took their name from their leader, calling themselves Amish-Mennonites, or the Amish.

Reading these stories made me feel like a detective on the hunt. The clues were cataloged, the motives clear—I just needed to figure out what it all added up to for me. And it was in the moment I realized Amish and Mennonite people *were* Anabaptists—that they lived the doctrines I so respected in Anabaptist culture—that I finally solved the mystery.

For these people weren't lost to history. They were around us, all over the country. *They* could be the community I'd been looking for.

After a lifetime of mistakes, I had located "my people" in a library. Now it was time to go out and find them in the real world.

For years I'd been aware that there was a tiny Amish community down in Sarasota called Pinecraft, about two miles from Darren's parents' house. Before, it had held little interest for me, but now, after connecting the Amish with Anabaptist doctrine, suddenly Pinecraft was the most important place in the world. It was like reading a family tree and realizing you have cousins living down the block. I just had to see it for myself.

So the first weekend I could manage it, Jacinda, Shannon,

Tyler, and I headed a hundred miles south on I-75 toward Sarasota, toward a new era in our life. We found Pinecraft by memory, and I shrieked with delight when we turned onto Bahia Vista Street and I caught my first glimpse of an Amish girl on a bicycle. Then I noticed a group of Amish women chatting blithely in the street. They were simple, and unabashedly so. I immediately sensed that in *this* place, I would never have to defend or apologize for my life choices.

We were looking for a church, any church, where we could attend service that morning. I was trusting in God to show us the way. We drove up and down slender lanes lined with white ranch houses, quaint rows of manicured green grass, and square garden plots.

Then suddenly Jacinda yelled from the backseat, "There! An Amish girl! Let's ask her where to go!"

The Amish girl was dressed in light-blue fabric and walking a green, old-timey Schwinn bicycle down the street. I slowed the van as we pulled up next to her.

"Excuse me?" I said from the window.

"Ya?"

A sweep of blond hair fell across her face. I asked, "Do you know where the church is?"

"What church are ya looking to go to?"

This was awkward. I didn't know. "Um . . . your church?"

"Oh," she said. "Okay. Well, I guess that's fine. If you want to follow me I can show you where it's at." She pointed down the road. "It's just a bit up there around the corner."

"Thank you," I said.

She hopped on her bicycle, then we putt-putted behind her, going a shade over five miles an hour, down the lane and across a busy intersection. We probably looked ridiculous.

We followed her to Pinecraft Amish Church, a gray stone building tucked behind a wedge of palm trees on the corner of

Hines Avenue and Clarinda Street. There were no other cars in the churchyard.

I parked near the street and turned around to my children.

"Now, we're going to behave in here, right?"

They nodded.

Jacinda asked, "But what about your shoes?"

"What?"

"Mom, I think you forgot your church shoes."

Oh no. I turned to Shannon. "Did you happen to grab my shoes before we left the house?"

"Nope."

Great. Here I was about to attend my first church service in a respected, four-hundred-year-old Christian institution, and I was going to walk in wearing sandals.

"Well," I said, "it's fixed now. There's nothing I can do. We'll just see if they let me in. Come on, let's go."

The girls hopped out of the van. I had to help Tyler get out of his car seat, and while I was fiddling with the straps, I heard Shannon whisper—

"Mom! Look."

I turned.

In every direction, a steady stream of placid, gray-haired Amish bicyclists were descending on the churchyard like the slowest ambush in recorded history. The men wore sharp black pants and vests with white shirts, brown shoes, straw hats, and gray beards; the women wore ankle-length dresses, white head coverings, and deep smiles. Most of them were middle aged, and very well fed.

"Don't stare," I whispered, hoisting Tyler into my arms.

Then we walked from our modern van back in time, into a world that I'd only experienced from the comfort of a library.

Inside the church, the first thing I noticed was the look of the women's faces. None of them wore makeup. And yet, their cheeks glowed with an unmistakable fire, a beauty that doesn't come from a compact. Whatever they had, I knew I wanted it.

We hovered near the back of the church for a few anxious moments, unsure where we were supposed to sit. The women seemed to be gathering on one side of the room and the men on the other. Thankfully, an older man approached and motioned for us to follow him. He showed us to a spot in the middle of the congregation.

The service began a moment later. First we prayed, then we sang a few songs in German. I tried to mumble along with the melody as best I could—lucky for me the songs were very, very slow.

After the final song, the bishop stood for his sermon, and to my surprise he began speaking English. I knew from the books I'd read that Amish church sermons were usually given in German—most of the Amish came to America from Switzerland, and many still use a low-German dialect called "Pennsylvania Dutch" in the day-to-day—so I felt lucky to have picked an Amish church that spoke the same language I did.

The Bibles were still written in German, however, and when the bishop first asked us to find a specific passage, I had a hard time finding the right place. The woman seated behind us must have noticed. She leaned forward and gently pointed out where we were in the text. Then she gave me a soft pat on the back.

The service itself was lovely—but what a marathon! It lasted three hours. God must have been working on my children, especially Tyler, because they never complained, never misbehaved, and never asked once to go to the bathroom. All three sat next to me enrapt, transfixed as I was by this holy and mysterious place.

At the end of the service, the congregation spilled out into the hot Florida sun, and I kept my eyes peeled for the woman who'd helped me with the German Bible. I wanted to thank her.

I spotted her standing at the edge of the crowd, near the bike rack. I walked over.

"Hello," I said.

"Well, hi there." She was spry and sturdy, maybe fifty years old and silver-haired. "I'm Martha."

We shook hands lightly.

"I just wanted to thank you for your help today," I said. "I don't read German at all, and don't know what I would've done without you."

"Oh, it's nothing," she said, smiling. "Did you like the service?"

"I did—it was amazing."

"Well, good. I thought it was a very strong one today." Then she winked. "Good spiritual food to fill one's soul for a week."

"It's just so uplifting."

"Yes, light and easy—just like we do things in Pinecraft."

I laughed, and she touched my arm as if we were old friends. I took the moment of levity to ask her another question that had been on my mind.

"Martha, I'm confused about something."

"Yes?"

"I thought that in Amish churches, the sermons were given in German."

"Oh, they are in German."

"Always?"

"Yes, mostly."

Well, this was confusing. Unless I'd miraculously learned to speak German in the last hour, I was pretty sure what I'd heard during church was English.

"So ... why wasn't today's sermon in German?" I asked her.

"Today was a special case."

"Oh?"

She smiled brightly. "Yes. We saw you were here."

"Me?"

"That's right. And of course we couldn't do the whole thing so you couldn't hear it. So we changed."

I was floored. "But why?"

"We wanted you to be comfortable," she said. "And we can tell you're not Amish."

Unbelievable. A woman from the modern world shows up to their church, in a modern car, wearing sandals, with young children in tow—and the congregation alters ancient tradition on her behalf.

I could cry I was so impressed. For much of my life I had felt so unwelcomed, so alone. And yet these Amish folks accepted me without reservation.

"Come on, dear," Martha said, taking my arm in hers. "Let's not stand around like a couple of dairy cows. I'll introduce you to some of the others."

"Sure," I said. "Let me just tell my children where I'll be, okay?"

Martha smiled. "I'll be waiting right here."

I found Jacinda, Shannon, and Tyler huddling conspiratorially underneath a palm tree.

"Now listen here," I said, looking each of them in the eye. "Mom's going to walk around with that nice lady over there and talk to some people. You go play over there in the grass and stay out of trouble."

"Okay," they said in unison.

"And what was that second part?"

All together: "Stay out of trouble."

"Good. Get." They dashed off.

When I returned to Martha, she led me through the church-yard, introducing me to every person who attended Pinecraft

Amish Church. Nobody mentioned my car or my sandals. They all seemed happy to see me.

It was so much fun, in fact, that I plum forgot about keeping an eye on my children. That is, until my maternal instinct suddenly flared. It started with a slight tickling, just under the chin. Then the hair on my neck stood up. And when my ears began to throb, and I began to get that warning every mother knows—*Danger! Danger! Your children have a terrible idea!* I knew something bad was about to occur.

I turned around in mid-conversation and located Jacinda, who was standing six paces away from a large rubber ball. Across the yard, Shannon was jumping up and down. And then I saw the men in their Sunday best, leaning against their bicycles, the Amish bishop included. Shannon was directly in front of them.

"Oh no."

Jacinda started toward the ball, Shannon stood ready to receive it, and suddenly time slowed to a crawl: I see Jacinda charge forward, her legs pounding the soft grass. I push past Martha and reach out, but it's too late—Jacinda blasts the rubber ball high into the air. Shannon's eyes widen as the ball blots the sun. The women look. The men squint. Jacinda winces. Shannon closes her eyes as a spherical shadow passes over her face.

Then the Amish bishop turns and—*blammo!*—receives a flying rubber ball right to the face, knocking his Amish hat clear off his head.

The entire congregation turned from the bishop to me, and then back to him again. The silence deafening.

He blinked twice. Then he tilted his head to the right and rubbed his coarse hand over his chin. Scrunched up his nose. Finally, he threw back his head, and that man let out the biggest, deepest laugh that I've ever heard—

"Hahahahahahahah!!!!"

He laughed from his belly and from his chest and from the big red circle forming on his cheek. He roared back again and again, shaking like a car engine as he pointed to the ground.

"Well," he said, "it is a good thing that my head is not still in that hat!"

His words were so unexpected that they tore through the crowd, sending gales of relieved laughter shooting forth like a geyser. For a solid minute the crowd fell into hysterics, the women giggling as the men bent over at the waist, trying to catch a breath.

Jacinda and Shannon laughed harder than anybody, and as I watched my children fall to the ground in giggles and the families laughing along with them — as if we were all part of some raucous inside joke — I knew.

I'd found them.

These were my people.

Chapter 13

GOODBYE

"Goat's Milk and Chicken Eggs for Sale."

The headline in the Dade City newspaper didn't catch my eye, but the picture next to it said a thousand words. It featured a woman standing along a fence post in rural Florida, goats and chickens behind her. But it wasn't the scenery that interested me; it was the woman: She was wearing a cape dress and a head covering. She was exactly who I'd been looking for.

For weeks I had been trying to locate an Amish or Mennonite church close to our house in New Port Richey. Our visit to Pinecraft had been transformative, but Pinecraft was a hundred miles away, and I felt a need to immerse myself completely in a lifestyle and a culture that supported Christian values sunup to sundown—which wasn't practical if I had to drive two hundred miles round-trip every day.

This lady in the picture, however—she was definitely Plain. And the brief newspaper profile said her farm was on County Road 301, which was less than fifty miles east of New Port Richey. Still a long way, sure, but fifty miles was doable. I was willing to do what I needed to find the church right for me.

Unfortunately, the newspaper didn't list a specific address for the farm, and so my only hope was to drive up and down County Road 301 until we spotted the sign. It was a shot in the dark, but that's exactly how we had found Pinecraft Amish Church after all. I figured if God willed it, we would find our Plain people. And then, once we were at the farm, we would do ... what, exactly?

I didn't know for sure. But I had faith I'd figure it out.

It was autumn in Pasco County then, and as the children and I drove east, we delighted in the pumpkin patches blooming along the roads for miles and miles. I always loved pumpkins—they bloom just when everything else is dying away. There's a little bit of symbolic hope stored up in those orange vegetables. I was hoping for a little late-blooming magic myself.

First, however, we had to find the farm, and as we approached County Road 301, an eight-lane highway, I realized I had no idea which way I should turn.

"Didn't you try and call them?" Tyler asked from the backseat.

Shannon, sitting in front, gently scolded her younger brother. "They don't have phones, silly."

"They do have phones, Shannon," I interjected. This was, and still is, a common misperception of many Plain cultures. "They're not exactly the same as the Amish people we met in Pinecraft. These are Mennonites, and this particular Mennonite group is a bit more modern. It said so in the newspaper. I would've called them, but information didn't have a number listed."

"Oh, okay," Shannon said. "So the best we can do is keep our eyes open, right, Mom?"

I was about to answer yes when I realized that driving around blindly was not, in fact, the best we could do.

"Well, we do have one other option," I said. "Let's ask God where to go."

I pulled our van into a gas station near the ramp for County Road 301. Then I turned around to face my children.

"Okay, now bow your heads." They closed their eyes.

I prayed, "Dear Lord, please help us find the Mennonite lady that we're looking for. We're searching for Your guidance in finding a Plain church. I know there must be one closer to our home than Sarasota, and I pray You'll show us the way. In Your name we pray, amen."

"Amen," said the kids.

"Right," I said.

"Right what?" asked Shannon.

"We're going right." A clear signal had leapt into my heart.

Jacinda spoke up. "You know which way already?"

I flicked on the van's blinker and shrugged. "We prayed. God said. So let's go."

As I pulled out of the gas station, I could hear Jacinda mutter from the backseat, "Boy—He sure acts fast."

He does indeed, because not more than a mile down Country Road 301 we spotted a sign for "Country Eggs and Goat's Milk."

"It's the farm!" Tyler yelled. "The farm! Turn, Mom!"

I'd already driven past the turn-in, so I yelled, "Hold on!" and crushed the brakes. We skidded to a stop. Then I backed up ten feet along the road and pulled into the mouth of the driveway.

"You all ready?" I asked.

They nodded, "Yep."

"Well, okay. Here we go."

I drove us down a bumpy and potholed rustic lane that led up to a small white house with a wooden porch. The land around us was wild and wooly and thick as a jungle—prime central Florida brush. I parked several feet from the porch. Looking up, I could see a dim figure behind a screened-in front door.

"Okay," I said to the kids, "let's be on our best behavior."

I felt a little uneasy stepping into the hot sun; this was a stranger's property, and I had no idea what I was about to say. But I was determined to find God's place for me.

When the screen door opened, a short man, maybe sixty years old, walked out onto the porch.

"Hi, there," he said. "Can I help you with somethin'?"

I didn't know how to start. "We, uh ... we saw your article in the paper."

"Oh ... yep, that'd be my wife's doin'. Unfortunately she's out of town this week, gone off to Oregon to see some family. But if you need some produce I can get it for you."

"Sure ... I mean no — we don't need any milk or eggs exactly."

"You don't?"

"No."

He scratched his head. "Well, what do you need?"

I looked at my children for support. "I ... well, we ..." Shannon nodded her encouragement. It was time to put my cards on the table.

"Sir, we're looking for a church."

"A church?"

"Yes — a Mennonite church."

"Mennonite."

"Yes, or at least I think so. The truth is, I saw your wife's picture in the newspaper, and she was wearing a cape dress, and I thought that maybe if I found her ..."

"Yes?"

"... then I might find her church."

The idea didn't sound as good in front of this man as it had in our kitchen. For a brief moment, I was afraid he might kick us off his land.

"Where are you all from?" he asked.

"New Port Richey," I said.

"That's forty miles!" he exclaimed, a big grin spreading over his face. "You came all the way out here just to find some church?"

"Yes."

He leaned against the porch and stroked his chin. "Well ... we do have a good one out here."

A ray of hope.

"And y'all are welcome to come to our church anytime. We love visitors. I'm not sure if it's what you're looking for, exactly, but it is Mennonite, and the people there are awfully nice." He waved at my car. "Those your children?"

"Yes sir."

"Well, they're cute ones. I tell you what—why don't you come back out here this Sunday? My wife'll be back by then, and you can ride over to church with us. We'll show you around and all."

I couldn't believe it. This day was unfolding just like one years ago—the day I'd walked into Power 106, completely unannounced, and wound up with a job offer. Back then I was a bleach-blond girl in a tight dress, and I'd turned down the opportunity because it would require me to be someone other than myself.

Now, I stood in a plain dress with curly hair, three children in my car. And my new offer would bring me one step closer to the woman I was supposed to become.

"We'd love to attend church with you next Sunday," I said. "And thank you so much for your kindness, Mr...."

"Mel. Just call me Mel."

I smiled. "Thank you, Mel."

"Well, a person's got to be nice to others, don't they? Especially people comin' all the way out here to get some church. What's your name anyway?"

"Sherry."

"Well, okay, Sherry. You come on back out here on Sunday and we'll get you where you need to get."

"That sounds wonderful."

I walked back to the car and we pulled away, but as I was passing the front porch, I spotted Mel yelling something to me from the railing. I rolled down the car window.

"What was that?" I asked

"I said, 'You sure you don't want any goat's milk?'"

"Not today." I shrugged. "Maybe another time?"

He grinned. "Sounds good."

Mel's church, Pleasantview Mennonite Fellowship, was a small congregation of six Mennonite families living way out in the Pasco County brush.

On the day my children and I returned to Mel's farm, he introduced his wife, Martha—the woman from the newspaper article—and his daughter-in-law, Monica, whose daughter Jodi was four years old. I couldn't help but notice a particularity of Monica's cream dress. It was *identical* to her daughter's. Down to the seam.

And then, as we arrived at Pleasantview, I saw that Monica and her daughter weren't the only ones whose clothes matched; every mother and daughter wore identical dresses. It was a Mennonite tradition found at many congregations, and a wonderful sight—family bonds expressed through clothes, a physical extension of lineage and love.

Inside the small white church, we began the service with a song, and once again I was entranced by those Old World hymns. They were sung a cappella—most Anabaptist churches view instrumentation as too "worldly"—and they were sung very slow. It felt like an ancient rhythm, a primordial tempo in lockstep with my heart.

Pump pa pa, pump pa pa.

And the melodies! They filled my throat and burrowed deep within my chest. Pump pa pa, pump pa pa.

After a personal and uplifting sermon from the bishop, the service ended with a prayer, and Martha introduced me to her family and friends. I could tell they were a people at peace and committed to God.

My children enjoyed themselves too. They quickly made

friends, and when we left later that afternoon, all three said they couldn't wait for the next Sunday to come around. I promised them we would return, and we did. And then we went the next week, and the week after that.

Soon I was even driving out to Mel's farm on the occasional afternoon. The children would play with the animals while I chatted with my new friends. Monica and I became especially close; I soaked up her spirit like a sponge. She had such strength of character, such kindness, that the whole world seemed safe and good when I sat by her side.

She told me stories from her Amish-Mennonite life as we sipped iced tea on the porch swing. She taught me to bake bread from scratch. She taught me how to focus all my energy on Christ, and on community—which she considered the foundation of a well-spent life.

"The church is like a back brace," she said to me. "In the beginning, your muscles are weak, and it is very hard to stand up straight. So you have to use the church, use those who love and support you, to grow stronger. Then one day you'll stand upright, and you'll find that you don't need the brace any longer. But that is still only the beginning, because the most important part is still to come."

"What part is that?" I asked.

"Only when you are standing upright and tall yourself, can you lean over and help brace the person next to you."

They were beautiful words. It was a beautiful time in my life. My friendship with Mel, Martha, and Monica, along with the welcoming arms of Pleasantview Mennonite Fellowship, made me feel as if I was nearing the end of a long journey.

I knew who I was, and I knew that my children would never have to struggle with the same fragmented identity I once had. Tyler, Shannon, and Jacinda would grow up stable and firm, confident in their values and believing in the redemptive power of Christ's love. All three enjoyed our Plain lifestyle, and they even looked to continue it when I wasn't around.

Every other weekend, my girls saw their father while visiting with their grandparents, and on Sundays, Darren's mother — who'd become a wonderful grandmother and friend since I'd left Darren, graciously dropped Shannon and Jacinda off at Sunnyside Church, of which Pleasantview was an extension, for Sunday service. Once my girls began attending Sunnyside, they returned to New Port Richey after every weekend feeling refreshed and whole.

I thought for a while that I'd finally found my place at Pleasantview. I daydreamed what my life would be like during long evenings with Martha on her porch, the two of us watching amber days give way to dusk. It had the right spiritual focus. It had the right people. It had the right feeling.

God's Plan *is* a mystery, though, and impossible to predict. I would soon learn this myself. I would also learn that I wasn't done starting over just yet.

I first realized that I had a tough choice to make on an otherwise pleasant day, when Martha offered to show me her community's one-room schoolhouse. I was interested in what sort of schools Amish and Mennonite children attended.

Somehow, she and I fell into a conversation about marriage. She told me a story about a family who'd previously lived in her community, a family who'd faced a difficult decision when the wife and husband became convicted that their marriage was not a spiritual union. The husband had been previously married, Martha explained, and both husband and wife interpreted the Bible's message as one that discouraged divorce and remarriage.

"What did they decide?" I asked my friend.

"They spent two years here seeking God's will," Martha said, "and ultimately felt a burden too great to continue their marriage. They separated, and she moved her family to a Plain community in Georgia."

"And the father?"

"He continued to support his family financially and emotionally—but from afar."

Martha had no idea how close this story paralleled my own, nor the burden I'd been feeling on account of it. I had made a specific vow, years before, with Tyler in my arms and a Bible in my lap, to do whatever God asked of me. I had promised Him that I would listen to my heart and let it guide me to Christ.

And my heart had been hurting. I didn't know God's Plan for me, but I knew that He revealed Himself through the Holy Spirit, and so, as I'd grown more burdened over my own remarriage to Toby, I had no choice but to take that burden seriously. It was, after all, the way God communicated His wishes for my life.

I needed to live fully immersed in a lifestyle committed to God. I wanted my whole being wrapped up in it, sunup to sundown, because that wrapping was my only defense against a slide back into darkness. I just couldn't risk that hole opening up in my heart again, and so I made a choice. I knew deep down it was the right one for me.

Toby and I ended our marriage soon after.

Somehow he understood that I was drawing a spiritual circle around myself because I couldn't live any other way. And he chose to be my brace. He would allow me to leave, to find my place, and to live as I knew I must.

And he would do it with a smile. As my friend.

Chapter 14

BEAT THE BULL

For many people, even many Christians, the decision to end my marriage to Toby might not make any sense at all. But all of us make personal choices difficult for others to comprehend. That's what makes being human so interesting—the ability to sympathize with, and have compassion for, people wholly different from us.

Why does a monk live on a mountain? Why does an Amish man drive a buggy?

It's because they feel compelled, and though the rest of us may not make the same choice with our own lives, we can accept the legitimacy of those decisions because we all make decisions like them. We all follow the truth our hearts lay out for us. My heart laid a truth out for me, and I followed it. I felt compelled. I made a spiritual choice that was hard to make, just like I did when I became a Christian. And I've never regretted either.

Toby and I divorced amicably with an understanding that he would always be a part of our lives. He still is today, nearly fifteen years after our divorce. We talk on the phone three or four times per week. His relationship with Tyler, Shannon, and Jacinda remains strong. He is a father figure to them, a position he earned by caring, by visiting whenever possible, and by encouraging them throughout the years.

It was Toby who eventually suggested the girls and I move down to Sarasota so we could be closer to Sunnyside

Church—which Shannon and Jacinda loved—and be closer to their grandparents.

So in search of a fresh start—and with wonderful memories of Pinecraft fresh in my mind—I took the small amount of money I'd saved, and I rented a house in Sarasota. I got a job cleaning houses on Mondays and Tuesdays, and then on Thursdays and Fridays I spent twelve hours each day making noodles and baked goods to sell at a farmer's market. I made just enough money to eke by every month.

Though working took up the majority of my time, I also spent many hours with a man named Lester Gingerich, an elder statesman of sorts and the former bishop at Sunnyside. Brother Lester's heart was as big as an ocean. If you've ever driven through Florida and seen billboards asking people to call a free suicide hotline—well, that number goes to Brother Lester. He listens. He feels. He answers people's questions with the Bible. He knows people need love, and he gives them all he's got.

He shared that love with my family too. He took an instant shine to us. I think he found something sacred in my story of conversion. Miraculous even. He loved the idea that a woman from the world might choose a Plain life—*could* choose a Plain life—through the power of God's love. He often encouraged me to tell my story to others.

In Brother Lester I found a mentor, and he would make an enormous impact on my life. It is ironic then, that the first time he truly helped me, he did so by helping to send me away.

I was looking for something more specific, some way of living that could support my spiritual evolution. It needed to be different than anything I'd experienced before—insular, like a cocoon, so I could continue to transform. One day I might even emerge a butterfly. Or at least a moth.

I often discussed my options with Brother Lester, and though he counseled me to live in Sunnyside, he also promised to help me any way he could. So when I asked him for a favor, he didn't hesitate. I'd heard about a community in Kentucky called Marrowbone, a place that seemed perfect for my plans, and I asked Brother Lester if he'd write my family a letter of introduction. He said he would be happy to do so.

Little did I know that Kentucky would soon challenge my family to the limits of survival. It would introduce us to hardships we'd never imagined. Marrowbone would make for a different sort of living. It was rural. It was Southern.

It was Amish.

We arrived in February on a bitingly cold day—a thermometer on the main gate said 4 degrees. Our defroster couldn't keep up with the chill, and I could barely see out the front windshield. I wiped at the condensation with my left hand and drove with the right, while keeping my eyes on the small trailer just ahead of us. That was our new home. It sat on a slight ridge in the middle of a cow pasture, billowing snow threatening to blow it all away.

When I pried open the trailer's front door a gust of frigid wind nearly took it from its hinges, and I quickly pushed the children inside. Then darkness. There were no overhead lights, just a thin ray of light peaking in from a back window. Behind the trailer there was an outhouse. Never saw something like that at Fred Segal's. Cracks in the outhouse wood paneling swallowed gusts of wind; I figured the chipboard seat had to be colder than the hull of an arctic trawler.

It was late in the day and light was fading, so I lit a small fire and the four of us—Shannon, Jacinda, Tyler, and I—wrapped ourselves in a thick comforter. I was afraid. I already wondered if I'd made a terrible mistake. Who trades palm trees for this?

Booooooooooummmpppp. Crick crick.

My eyes shot open. Must've fallen asleep. It was dark outside.

Boooooummmmmmp. Crick.

I checked my watch. It was 3:30 a.m.

Criiiick. Crick Crick. Criiiiick.

"Jacinda!" I hissed under the comforter. "What is that?!"

Booooooooommmmpp.

She slid out from under the fabric. "I don't know."

It came again, louder—a creaking, guttural noise moving up and over the outside of our new home.

"Mom, I'm scared."

"I know. Me too. Wake your sister."

I eased out of bed and crept into the kitchen. Next to the stove I found a small hatchet hanging on a nail. I grabbed it and scurried back to Jacinda.

"Here," I said, thrusting the hatchet into her pale hand.

"What am I supposed to do with this?"

"I have no idea."

Shhrrcchh Shhhrrccchh Shhrrccchhh.

It was lower now, almost at the floorboards.

"Please don't be a puma," I thought to myself. Then, to Jacinda—"Do they have pumas in Kentucky?"

Shannon pulled the comforter from her face. "Mom, they have black bears in Kentucky."

Great. Bears. We've left city life to be mauled by bears.

A loud *bump* suddenly shook the trailer. Jacinda clutched at the hatchet. Shannon pulled the covers back over her head.

"Stay calm," I said to both them, or to myself—I didn't know which. "Jacinda, watch your sister. I'm gonna look outside."

Slowly and with total dread, I tiptoed past the king-size bed, past the little pile of toys the girls took everywhere, and to the bay window.

"Please don't be a bear," I thought, "or a drunk man or a puma."

I pulled the curtain aside and leaned in. The glass was fogged, so with quiet hands I rubbed an oval large enough for two fearful eyes. Then I took a deep breath ... and I looked.

"It's cows!" I yelled out. "Cows!"

"Huh?"

"The cows!" I whispered, motioning for the girls to come see. "Hurry!"

Shannon bolted from the comforter as Jacinda, hatchet still in hand, flopped across the wood floor in loose flannel pajamas. They huddled next to the window.

"There," I pointed, and there it was, our monster: a lazy-eyed cow rubbing its impressive hind end against our trailer.

"Can he see us?" Jacinda asked.

"No, honey."

Just then the cow let out the lowest, groaniest moo ever heard; it sounded like a tugboat foghorn.

"Mmmmmmmmmoooooooooooooo!"

"What's going on?" Tyler asked, suddenly awake.

Jacinda turned. "A cow is rubbing his rear on our house."

"Oh," he said.

Then he turned over and went right back to sleep.

The morning after our run-in with that impressively hind-ended cow, my family and I ventured timidly into our new world to take stock of the land—a large pasture enclosed in high fencing.

A man named Roy owned the property. He lived further up the ridge, and a few months earlier he'd allowed a young Amish man named Laverne Sensenig to place a trailer in his cow pasture and live inside. Laverne had moved to Marrowbone to properly court his beloved Laura, and when they were married, the couple moved to a house in the community. The trailer had been unoccupied ever since—until we came along, that is.

Jacinda and Tyler loved the place. There was a guinea chicken coup in the backyard, a small pond down in the glade, and enough cows, horses, dogs, and cats to fill a children's book. Tyler already dreamed about the frogs, fish, snakes, and fowl he could catch by summer. Shannon was a little more reserved. She was a girl's girl, and to her, all of Kentucky seemed made of either snow or mud. And she hated mud.

I didn't mind how the property looked, because I wanted my family to learn how to survive. We only had a few hundred dollars to live off of every month, which meant we would have to become self-sufficient. If we couldn't raise it, make it, or grow it—then we'd go without it.

Thankfully, we had help from the people in our new community. Many of them stopped by to say hello. They were so excited to add a new and exotic last name to the community roll. "Gore" wasn't exactly Amish. Some of the women even brought us freshly baked bread and treats.

And none of them seemed to care that my family had lived in the modern world for most of our lives either. Once again, the Plain people offered me the type of unconditional acceptance I'd always longed for. Fannie, a woman who would help me set up my first business, even told Tyler to "hurry up and wear out those pants so I can sew you a pair of broadfalls." (Broadfalls are traditional cotton trousers with no zippers, usually worn with suspenders.)

As I spent those first few days with my new neighbors, I also learned more about the Marrowbone community itself—a tiny Amish settlement nestled in the crook of Kentucky's great Cumberland River. It was a quirky place. They weren't New or Old Order Amish exactly, and so they didn't prescribe to a set standard of living. Some of the more progressive people used electric mixers to make Amish treats, while others did without electricity entirely. They held church services in English, and unlike many traditional Amish communities, they were mission-minded, meaning they often traveled out into the world to share their love of Christ.

There were nineteen families in all, including mine, and

each one had come to Marrowbone from a different part of the country. It was a melting pot, an Amish gumbo; in Marrowbone there was a place for everyone. Maybe that's why I felt it was the right place for me.

We received a lot of help from our new community early on because I was considered a *graus* widow—a married woman who no longer lived with her husband. I was appointed a pair of overseers, a long-held tradition in Amish culture, who were tasked with helping us keep wood in the stove, food in the pantry, and clothes on the children. My overseers were a nice couple with no children of their own. I was happy to have their help because it wasn't too long before I realized the primary difference between living in New Port Richey and living on a farm in Kentucky—everything would be more difficult.

Mornings, the guinea-chicken coop blared to life before dawn, tossing us out of bed with an earsplitting squawk. We'd eat breakfast at a small wooden table next to the bay window, and then I'd prepare to "beat the bull." See, there was a mean old pink-butted white bull, a Charolais, that kept vigilant watch over the dirt lane leading from our trailer to the main gate. He never once tried to make friends with me, and so anytime I had to get anywhere on our property, I had to get there despite his best efforts.

Hence, "beat the bull." I'd stretch my legs, wipe my hands, and then sprint out of the house and down the dirt lane, hoping to reach our swing gate before that bull reached me. It was terrifying, but I had no choice—he only chased after me. Not my children, not our guests. Only me.

And I have to say, I must have some Basque blood in me somewhere, because just as those Spaniards outrun those bulls in Pamplona, I beat my bull every time.

Once I was up and over the swing gate, I could walk on the other side of the fence to anywhere I wanted to go on the farm. Often, that bull would follow me down the line for a bit. I always took the chance to gloat.

"You aren't so tough," I'd say through the fence. He would huff and puff, flare his nostrils, and kick at the dirt, but he knew who was boss. Eventually he'd sulk back to his perch in defeat.

After I'd beaten the bull a few times in the morning, it was usually time to do the laundry with my ringer washer, which would freeze up on the coldest days, or make lunch for my girls, who by noon were just arriving home from Amish parochial school. Then in the afternoon I'd read stories to Tyler or hunch over whatever small craft—usually a rug—I was making to sell at the local auction house. Often Dorothea, our neighbor's daughter, would help me sew. If we needed a snack, I'd whip up some bagels and cream cheese or a pot of "Mexican" hot chocolate (the trick is to add cinnamon). Then it was usually time to start dinner and go to bed.

And those nights! Even after I moved us out of the trailer and into a house, the nights were so unimaginably cold. We'd huddle under flannel sheets dressed in our snow boots, jackets, gloves, and hats. On the coldest nights I would sleep on the floor, wrapped in a wool army blanket, waking every hour to add kindling to the fire.

I have to say the harsh conditions did what I hoped they would. We grew strong in Kentucky; we learned we could do anything we put our minds to. If it was freezing outside and the fire wouldn't stay lit, we didn't call a handyman—we burned furniture. Or books. I hated the latter, but sometimes it was all we had.

We also learned to help one another. In Florida I ran the house by myself while the children played, but in Kentucky, Jacinda and Tyler worked the land or helped neighboring farmers while Shannon helped me cook without modern appliances. My family became a four-wheeled wagon trundling up a hill—if one wheel didn't roll, the whole wagon stopped. Our days and nights were long and sometimes brutal, but every night when we plopped down into bed, utterly exhausted, there awaited us a small feeling of victory. We'd made it another day. We'd survived.

I didn't miss the modern world. I didn't miss the stress of having money or material things or the constant anxieties. I didn't miss traffic or getting irritated in line at the grocery or constantly monitoring the pop culture my children were soaking up. I didn't miss how the phone rang constantly or how one phone call from the wrong person could ruin an otherwise pleasant afternoon.

In the modern world I felt as if I was always rushing somewhere: to pick up the kids, to get away from someone, to go somewhere, to find something, to make a deadline, and so on.

Time marched at a different pace in our Amish community. We lived as slow as our songs in church. Our news was delivered by mail or word of mouth. I spent hours watching clouds or doing chores. And again, each night—that feeling of wearied and yet satisfied rest. I never slept so well in my life.

We were living an Amish farm-fed life. It was as if I'd taken the one bright spot in my adolescence, my idyllic summer in Escondido, and rebuilt it for my children to enjoy. And in our new environment, each of us bloomed, unearthing new abilities and latent talents we might not have discovered otherwise.

Shannon proved herself a whiz in the kitchen and around the house, presaging her future life as a wife, mother, and all-around household supervisor. Tyler took his adventurousness to new heights, earning a part-time job catching snakes and selling them to a physician, and helping neighbors at harvest. Jacinda began raising livestock and in no time built a small business buying and selling goats, geese, chicken eggs, and sheep.

And me? I was going in directions previously thought

inconceivable. My new friends in Marrowbone encouraged me to earn money doing something I enjoyed, and their encouragement led me down a professional path I'm still on today. In Marrowbone, I learned how to make chocolates and fudge. In Marrowbone, I learned how to write.

There were several friends that helped me along: Noah and Fannie Yoder, Jerry and Joanna Williams, Uri and Martha Byler. And then there was the Esh family.

I was drawn to John Esh, the father, from the first time I spoke with him. I saw in his personal story many elements of my own. Like me, he had once struggled to find his place.

John had grown up in an Old Order Amish community. For most of his life he figured he would die there too. But then, in his mid-forties, he'd found his heart moved to spread God's Word, putting him at a spiritual crossroads. Mission work was discouraged in John's Old Order Amish community, so he was forced to make a choice: follow his heart or follow his tradition.

He chose to follow his heart, becoming baptized into a more progressive Amish church. Unfortunately his new way of living came into conflict with his Old World community, and he was asked to leave the only place he had ever called home. He chose Marrowbone as his place to start over.

I couldn't believe the similarities between John's story and my own. Of course, he had been born into an ancient world, and I a contemporary one—but we shared the same journey to faith. We both made choices people couldn't understand. We both put our love of God and our search for His calling above all else. We both followed our heart.

And as John, his wife, Sadie, and I spent more time together, they supported my spiritual journey more and more. They became one of those "back braces" Monica had told me about.

Sadie supported me through friendship, inviting my family to her famous "mystery dinners," where the menu was kept secret and guests randomly selected which utensils *could not* be used during the meal. And John, himself a minister, supported me through his faith, always reminding me that, "Jesus Christ is the one who provides us our bounty and our capacity for joy."

My children too drew support from the Esh family. Rachel, the youngest daughter, attended school with my girls. Abner Esh taught their class. Betty Esh taught Tyler. Johnny Esh took Tyler on his first turkey hunt.

They were some of our closest friends in Marrowbone, so it shouldn't be surprising that the Esh family had a unique part in two instances where I planted seeds for my future professional life.

The first instance was centered around — what else — food.

I'd mostly stayed clear of sweets in my younger days, but when my children came along, I found I loved baking them tasty treats, and brownies, cookies, and cakes became a staple in our home. Over time I grew into a strong cook with many techniques at my disposal.

So as I began to consider how I might earn a living in Marrowbone, baking immediately came to mind. Wouldn't my desserts sell? Couldn't everybody use a little more sugar?

I figured they could.

At first, Shannon and I made fudge and hand-dipped choco-lates to sell at the farmer's market on Saturdays. We used fresh cream from a cow my friend Fannie owned and fresh butter that Tyler helped make by vigorously shaking cream in a mason jar. The candies were delicious, and they sold extremely well, but it wasn't until Rosanna Esh, Sadie's daughter-in-law, taught me to make fried pies that our operation really took off.

Shannon would make the fillings — a delicious blend of sugar, apple schnitz (dried apples), and butter — and pack the pies, while I stood at the stove frying them up. We made the dough from scratch and couldn't afford to waste an inch. Our goal was to turn out a hundred pies a day, three days per week, plus all the fudge and hand-dipped chocolates we were making before.

It was such a mess! The finished pies were too soft to stack one on top of another, and so on "baking days" my entire kitchen overflowed—from table to countertop, cabinets to chairs—with individually wrapped fried pies and fudge. Dried dough covered every kitchen handle. Flour handprints covered every wall.

Then on Saturdays I would ride out to the farmer's market and hawk our pies for $1.25 each.

It was hard work but it was fun work; after all, somebody had to taste each batch for quality control. And I have to admit that, in those days, I ate a lot of pie.

Our baking business earned enough money for us to survive long-term in Marrowbone, and so that's where we stayed. Shannon and Jacinda finished their first year at school and then started another. Tyler, who'd had a BB gun in his hand from the first day we'd arrived in Kentucky, turned eight, and I bought him a rifle so he could shoot squirrels, rabbits, and frogs that we cooked up and ate.

Every Sunday we attended Marrowbone Church—a brand-new meeting house with wood planks for flooring and two-hundred-year-old pews—and then on weeknights we visited the Esh family, or my friend Fannie, or any one of the other nineteen families that made up our simple community at the crest of the Cumberland River. Life was good.

Life in Kentucky was also very, very interesting.

There was the time Tyler escaped a white mule by jumping into a barbwire fence and I found him hanging from his broadfalls. When I confronted the mule it tore the broom from my hand and ran away. The next morning, I found four inches of handle lying on my porch. The mule had eaten the rest.

Carl Harris with
me on his lap
• • • • •

Me and my
brother Wayne
• • • • •

Ninteenth
birthday
• • • • •

Me (age 19) with
Somara and April

• • • • •

First family photo
taken of all four
siblings together,
1985. Left to right:
Wayne (17), April (7),
Somara (9), me (20)

• • • • •

Toby's and my
wedding, May 1995.
Back (left to right):
Somara, me, April,
Toby. Front (left
to right): Jacinda,
Shannon, cousin Joe

• • • • •

My baptism at First Baptist Church of Jasmine Lakes by Pastor Francis. (September 1996)

• • • • • • •

Tyler riding a horse

• • • • •

Shannon, Tyler, and Jacinda on "moving day", 2002.

• • • • •

Jacinda caring for our horse.

• • • • •

Going for a buggy ride, a common
sight while we lived in Kentucky

• • • • •

Then there was the story of my wagon, a sad but sturdy old thing. It didn't have a bench installed in the bed, and so when I drove the girls around, we'd just toss a couple of loose chairs in the back. I'd slap the horse's reigns, the wagon would rumble down the road, and the girls would jitter back and forth across the floorboard—one hand on their chairs and one hand on their head coverings—as if I'd devised the strangest method for training bull riders in history.

And the storm! It came on the heels of a long afternoon while we were at my friend Arden Miller's house. A big rainy hailstorm came through as we left and the sky turned green. Wind ripped the umbrellas from our hands, and hail the size of nectarines pelted our heads so mercilessly I was forced to pull over at the side of the road. I prayed for God to deliver us safely home, and right then a friendly man in a pickup truck offered to drive my children to the house. I agreed, but I still had the horse to deal with, so I fought through the devilish rain alone, drenched clothes clinging to me like a frightened child. Only when I was safe in our living room did I learn that a devastating tornado had touched down in Marrowbone, and that I had essentially driven right through its path.

Yes, we cultivated a bushel of wild tales in Kentucky. It almost seemed selfish to keep them all to myself, and so I began to write them down in letters to my Amish and Mennonite friends back in Florida. Sometimes the best parts of my weeks were spent reliving those stories in my mind as I licked envelopes and sent them away.

And apparently my friends in Florida enjoyed reading my letters as much as I enjoyed writing them, because they forwarded my letters to their own friends, who then forwarded them to *their* friends. Why? I think many of them were curious about how we "city folk" managed to live on a farm. Or maybe they were nostalgic about their own Amish upbringings. Some were probably just intrigued by Marrowbone itself. In any case, about a year after I began to write down my stories, I found out they were circulating the Plain world like an Amish viral video.

At first I was bashful about it, but then I realized I could use our stories to show how God was influencing our family. And as I focused more and more on God, more and more people from across the country asked me for copies of my letters—so many, in fact, that I couldn't keep up with the demand. I tried to copy them by hand but found I became so sore I could hardly fold a fried pie into a skillet. I imagined there had to be better way.

And that, finally, is how the Esh family had a small part in my writing. Elmer Esh, John's son, had an interesting contraption in his house near the back.

It was a computer—a word processor to be exact.

Seeing that modern technology in an Amish house was just about the funniest thing I'd ever seen, and the irony of it didn't escape me as I sat down to type a letter for the first time.

My father had made a fortune on computers, after all. And now here we both sat, a computer and Sherry Gore—in the Amish world.

Chapter 15

CRACKED

The Marrowbone community accepted my family into their loving arms from the moment we moved to Kentucky, but that didn't mean we were always treated the same as everyone else. I was a *graus* widow, a somewhat rare designation, and we'd moved into an Amish community from the modern world, which was downright unheard of. Our friends and neighbors couldn't help but perceive us as outsiders, even after we'd lived in Marrowbone for nearly three years, because we *were* outsiders—much of the cultural shorthand was lost on us.

I first began to perceive slight cultural differences when I attempted to release our Amish overseers from their responsibilities. Shannon and I were doing well selling our pies by then, and with the extra money Jacinda earned raising and selling livestock, our family found itself on sound financial footing. I was becoming more comfortable bartering for goods and services, such as cutting meat for a farmer in exchange for thirty pounds of fresh hamburger, or canning vegetables for a discounted price on baled hay.

Those activities—earning and managing money, bartering for goods—were traditionally done by males in Amish society, and as I sought more control over those elements of our lives, my neighbors grew more concerned. It all boiled down to a clash of perspective. Everyone knew that as a *graus* widow I had no husband to perform those duties for me. That was a given. The question was what to do about it.

As a child of modern society, I was raised to value independence and personal freedom above all else. No man around to work the farm? Jacinda and I could do it. No man around to earn money? Shannon and I could start a baking business. I wasn't looking to make a statement. I felt I had no choice, and I believed in the maxim, "God does for those who do for themselves."

Many people in my community, however, grew up on Old Order Amish farms where fathers and mothers had specific roles to play. Deviation from those roles was generally discouraged. If there was no father in the house, as it was in my case, then the community traditionally took over the father's tasks.

It's actually a beautiful idea—a community pulling together to make up for the loss, or in my rare case, the absence, of a husband. I knew my Amish friends were just trying to relieve some of my burden. But I didn't grow up on those Amish farms, and I hadn't spent years building a new life for my family to just hand over the reins.

So I chafed at the specter of control, and over time I began to feel smothered. But the issue didn't really come to a head until it began to involve my children.

Our overseers thought Tyler suffered without a strong male voice in our household. They just couldn't believe I was capable of raising a boy without help. Obviously I disagreed, and our disagreement boiled over one particularly drab afternoon when I learned a boy and his brothers had chased Tyler with a whip and lashed him on the leg. Tyler had responded by tackling one of the boys.

When the rest of Marrowbone found out about the altercation our overseers were quickly dispatched to our home.

"What are you going to do?" they asked me.

"It's already been taken care of," I said. "I spoke with the boys' fathers, and we already got them together to apologize."

"And what about Tyler?"

"He apologized too."

"But what did you say about tackling the other boy?"

"Those boys picked a fight with him and he stood up for himself without hurting anybody. All in all, I think it was a pretty responsible decision."

I could tell they didn't agree with my verdict. "And what have you decided on for his punishment?" they added.

"There won't be any punishment. It's been resolved."

"Then how will he learn what he did was wrong?"

My overseers didn't have any children of their own, so I could excuse the assumption that children only learn through punishment.

"He's already learned," I told them. "He listened to me, and he feels sorry for what he did. He understands."

They shared a troubled look, and right then I realized we were at a cultural impasse. They were raised in a strict society where every action had a specific reaction, a black and white society with few shades of gray. I was raised in Orange County; the very name implies color. In this case it was a bridge too far. They lived only a few miles from me, but we were worlds apart.

After Tyler's fight, I asked my overseers to step away from their responsibilities, and, to their credit, they backed down. I'm sure there was some backstage handwringing amongst the elders. I'm sure they wished I would accept their "old ways," which had been tested for hundreds of years. But if there was one thing I'd learned from my late-in-life conversion to Christianity, it was that a person has to follow her heart. And my heart told me that I needed to teach my children to stand up for what they believed.

It was a lesson they understood. Soon Jacinda would face her own conviction, and her own choice—one that wasn't too dissimilar to one I'd made in my own life.

Jacinda was thirteen when she first began to seriously consider baptism. For her twelfth birthday, she'd asked for *Martyrs Mirror*, a 1,500-page history of Christian persecution and martyrdom — and read it cover to cover. She spent hours reading the Bible and thinking about its many layers. She knew she wanted to live her life as a Christian. All that was left for her was to make it official.

I still remembered my own baptism like it was yesterday — how clean I'd felt emerging from that water, how different the world had seemed when I awoke the next morning. I wanted those same things for her. It was a supreme gift to be accepted by the Lord, and when Jacinda told me she wanted to be baptized I felt so excited I almost couldn't stand it.

There would be one major difference between Jacinda's baptism and mine, however. While I had been baptized into a fairly standard Christian church, Jacinda would be baptized into an Amish-Mennonite church. I assumed it wouldn't be a problem. We loved Marrowbone. We loved its people. And Jacinda approached her baptism with a full heart and high hopes.

She would end the process feeling much different.

It was a strange time in our community to be embarking on such a sacred commitment. Marrowbone had been struggling for months to resolve a dispute over some of its standards of practice, and recently the community had resolved to transition into a Mennonite Church. The rules would be more lax. Men could wear watches. Women could wear veils.

Jacinda went into her baptism classes — traditional, weekly gatherings that deepen a young person's relationship with God and reinforce notions of personal accountability and community — already a bit confused as to why so many standards were being changed. It didn't make sense to her that the previous guidelines, which had been presented as God's Law, could be so swiftly thrown out for something new. And she had many questions about her church.

But during her first class, when she began firing questions at her teachers, they had no answers for her. They weren't prepared for such an intellectually curious child. They told her she was "too young to ask such things" and that "it wasn't right to question God."

Jacinda was incredulous. How could a person understand their faith if they couldn't ask about it?

She often came home from the classes dejected. And when the other girls began to ask Jacinda if she would ask *their* questions for them—most girls attended class with fathers at their side and were afraid to ask—Jacinda became frustrated even more.

Morning, noon, and night she prayed. She fasted four days leading up to her scheduled baptism. I could see she was struggling with some of the same thoughts I had when I left our Baptist church. Like me, she was trying to follow her heart. She was listening close to what God had to say.

Eventually her choice was made clear to her: she did not feel right being baptized into the Marrowbone church. She would wait, and she would commit to God on her terms. Or as she put it—on His.

I could certainly identify with her decision. I was happy she'd made it. But I also knew, from my own experience, the reaction some people would have to her choice. And unfortunately I was right.

Many in our close-knit Amish community were shocked; a person didn't turn down the Lord, and that's exactly how some of the more staunch members saw it—a rejection of faith. They couldn't see past her choice to the conviction behind it; they couldn't see her love for Christ. They only saw a reaffirmation of the perils of independence, that old Gore family bugaboo.

Furthermore, Marrowbone was buckling under the strain of its conversion to a Mennonite church. It wasn't long before one community became three. Some left for Pennsylvania. Others chose to settle in a New Order Amish church in Summertown, Tennessee. The rest stayed in Kentucky.

I couldn't make heads or tails of the split as it was taking place, but in hindsight, I guess the same quality that made our community great—its diversity—also had the capacity to sow seeds of ill will. The Amish have that in common with the rest of the world, I guess. What I found painful was that I'd moved to Marrowbone to escape that sort of divisiveness.

Plus, my family was now in a limbo of sorts. I wasn't interested in moving to Pennsylvania, and we weren't likely to fit in with the Summertown group; as a New Order Amish church they would hold service in German.

Staying in Marrowbone would be the trickiest solution of all. Jacinda's decision to refuse baptism meant she was no longer suited to stay, and her refusal pretty much meant I wasn't either. I wasn't yet a full member of the Marrowbone church, having never been baptized there; I'd initially waited to make sure the community was right for my family. Now, after the split, I wasn't so sure it was.

It was a sad day when we finally packed up and left Kentucky. It had been our home for nearly three years. We were leaving behind so many friends and memories, so much personal growth and change. I purposely avoided John Esh the whole week before we left because I was afraid that if I saw his face I wouldn't go. He was just too good a man to disappoint.

Living in Marrowbone had taught me how to fight, how to make do with what I had. And it was there that I watched each child of mine blossom.

Shannon, so bright and effervescent, who would one day marry a prince charming, learned in Kentucky that she was a girl's girl, a homemaker and mother-to-be who was made to smile through the darkest days.

Tyler found his moral compass out there in the Kentucky

fields. He would use it to grow into a strong-willed and tough young man, a hunter and fisherman as independent, loyal, and honest as a person can be—truly a person who could be counted on.

And finally, there was Jacinda. Her future was more complicated. In a way, she never left Kentucky. She emerged from her shell there, burned bright, and left an imprint I still see in my dreams: Jacinda, standing upright and tall next to a workhorse, brushing its mane in a light breeze.

She would lose much in the coming years. Her strength. Her energy.

But her soul is still free, and I know that sometimes it still races over those bountiful bluegrass fields of Kentucky, chasing chickens, goats, horses, and hens.

Full of life, and unaware of what was to come.

Chapter 16

DOOMSDAY
TUESDAY

When my family was struggling through that first Kentucky winter I thought those hardships might be the most difficult we would ever face. I figured God was throwing the worst at us so we could sharpen our faith habits to a fine point. So we could learn to live as Christian people.

And we did learn much. We incubated in Kentucky. Through labor and sacrifice, God showed us what we were capable of in body, mind, and spirit; He helped us build a strong spiritual foundation under our feet. We emerged ready to make new lives for ourselves.

But long before Marrowbone came asunder, back when even the possibility of leaving our Amish wonderland would've seemed wildly implausible, there was something keeping me up late at night. It started innocuously, but it would not stay that way. It would soon dwarf the travails of our Kentucky adventure, and develop into a crisis that would test the limits of my faith.

For it wasn't something that was happening to me. It was something happening to my child.

My family was attending a funeral in Florida the day Jacinda began experiencing severe back pain and vomiting. I took her to the ER, where I was told she had a kidney stone requiring surgery. A month later she had the operation, and I thought that was that. But then, not a month later—on Mother's Day no less—Jacinda grew violently ill, and I rushed her back to the hospital. Additional test results indicated she was suffering from a disease called ulcerative colitis (UC).

UC is an inflammatory bowel disease that tends to flare up in waves. A patient might be in remission for months, even years, before symptoms return, and the symptoms are often limited to mild discomfort. Jacinda took the news as well as a young girl can. She seemed eager to beat her illness. She continued raising animals, going to school, and playing with her siblings and friends. She just had to rest a little more, and when her UC symptoms flared, adjust her lifestyle accordingly.

But her medical problems didn't weaken over time, as our doctor suggested they might—not in the slightest. They grew more difficult every week that passed. By the time Jacinda was thirteen, she'd been treated for over twenty kidney stones, and her doctor, who was growing convinced something more insidious might be at play, sent her for a consultation at Vanderbilt University Hospital.

"I don't like some of the red flags I'm seeing," said our specialist at Vanderbilt after reviewing Jacinda's tests.

That term scared me to no end. "What do you mean 'red flags'?" I asked.

"Signs that might indicate something worse than mere kidney issues."

I wondered to myself what could possibly be worse than watching my hyperactive daughter stay in bed all day. But then I found out real quick.

"I suspect she has a tumor," the specialist said.

Tumor—such a nasty sounding word. I physically recoiled when he said it.

He continued, "We're going to have your daughter tested by an endocrinologist, do some more blood work, and that should give us a better picture of what's going on. But I want to be clear—this is very serious."

I fully understood how serious a possible tumor was. I left his office devastated. Then, on the following Tuesday, a date forever burned into my memory as "Doomsday Tuesday," I received news that, yes, Jacinda did have a growth. But it wasn't a tumor. Further MRI testing clarified it as a cyst growing on her pineal gland, right at the base of her brain.

"We're fairly sure it's benign," I was told. "But it's important for you to understand that a benign cyst can require surgery with the passage of time. You'll have to keep a close eye on her."

"But how will I know if she needs surgery?"

"Symptomatic changes, Ms. Gore. Anything out of the norm. Excessive vomiting that won't cease."

I couldn't believe what was happening. Stomach pains to kidney stones to ulcerative colitis to a cyst—and Jacinda was just thirteen. I prayed nightly for God to protect her.

It was relatively soon after we returned from Vanderbilt that we moved out of Kentucky, aiming for a small Anabaptist community located outside Winston-Salem in North Carolina. I would've preferred to have moved to another Amish community, but Marrowbone was unique in that it held church service in English. Any other Amish community that we might have moved to—especially on such short notice—would've held their service in German. And as for returning to Sunnyside, the children were a little uncomfortable being so near Darren at that time in their lives.

Plus, my goal had never been to seek "Amish" or "Mennonite" cultures specifically; it was Anabaptist doctrine I needed—head coverings, simple living, a literal interpretation of the Bible, etc. The community outside of Winston-Salem would do just fine.

I contacted my sister April about helping us get set in North

Carolina, and she loved the idea, so I drove down to Florida, where she was living with her two boys, and brought them back to the three-bedroom house I'd rented sight unseen.

April helped me so much during the short time we lived in North Carolina. She was the only person to whom I could confess my heartache over Jacinda's illness. I tried to keep a smile on my face for the children, but inside, I felt powerless and weak. I had no idea whether I had the strength Jacinda required, or what I would do should things go from bad to worse.

And unfortunately, that is exactly what things were about to do.

My two closest friends in North Carolina were named Richard and Tina, and in early September they dropped by our house for an afternoon visit. I was pulling a bright blueberry pie out of the oven when they arrived, so I called for the children to answer the door. Tyler shot out of his room like a rocket and plopped onto the couch. Shannon came in from the backyard and let our friends in the front door.

I stepped into the living room to say hi, and as soon as I saw Richard I knew something was wrong. He was looking at Jacinda, who'd managed to walk from her bedroom into the kitchen.

"Sherry, is Jacinda doing okay?" he asked me, his voice low.

I wiped my hands on a yellow dishcloth. "She can't keep much food down lately. Even water."

As soon as the words left my mouth, Jacinda leaned over the sink and threw up the water she'd been trying to drink.

"What does her doctor say about it?"

"That she has a kidney stone."

"Nothing else?"

"No."

He looked into the kitchen and then back to me. "Listen

Sherry, I'm no doctor, but she looks very sick to me right now—too sick to be here at home. I think you should take her to the hospital."

Curious, I took off my cooking apron and walked back into the kitchen. Jacinda turned to me, and what I saw made my knees buckle—Richard was right.

Her downward slide had been so incremental, so gradual, that only through Richard's perspective could I see her pale skin, her eyes dark like they'd blown a fuse. Her bones poked through her willowy form like a sack of tools.

I was astonished. My mind suddenly flashed back in time, to that terrible day at Vanderbilt Hospital.

"Look for symptomatic changes . . . ," the specialist had said.

I thought about how much pain she'd felt in the last week, how little food she'd kept down. And suddenly, I *knew*.

And I roared.

"Come on!" I said firmly, sprinting out of the kitchen. "We have to go."

I pulled Jacinda to her feet, then pivoted to Tyler, who was playing near the window.

"Tyler, go get washed up."

"Are we going somewhere?" he asked.

"Yes."

"What for?"

"*Now*, Tyler."

He glanced at Jacinda and then back to me. "Are we going to the hospital?"

"Yes."

Then he looked into my panicked eyes and said something I couldn't believe, something that stopped me cold: "But she's always like this."

I froze in front of him, my hands crimping the edge of his jacket as if it were a lifeline. *Would this be the way he would remember her? Sickly and weak?* I glanced at Shannon across the room. *Would she forget how Jacinda had bounded over the Kentucky fields?*

Jacinda's head covering sagged low on her forehead.

Would I?

"No," I said aloud. Then I turned back to Tyler, fell to my knees and grabbed him by the shoulders.

"Your sister is very sick right now, sicker than she has ever been before, and we're going to take her to the hospital so she can get better."

"How do you know she'll get better?"

I stroked his blond hair. "Because she has to."

Our back door opened and April came in from the yard. I quickly decided to leave my children with her and take Jacinda to the hospital alone. Richard helped me get Jacinda out of the kitchen, down the front steps, and into my van, and moments later we were speeding toward Brenner's Children's Hospital.

I drove in silence — then in horror as Jacinda began to spit up thick gobs of green and black bile. It was terrible. I was shaking by the time a bright-red Emergency sign came into view.

The ER nurse examined Jacinda in triage and immediately admitted her to a room, where I explained her case to the doctors on staff. They were very concerned. They felt Jacinda should stay the night so they could run tests in the morning. I called April and told her I wouldn't be home.

At ten o'clock the next morning, I was summoned from Jacinda's room to a consulting room down the corridor. I was in shock, certainly, but not particularly scared. After all, it couldn't be serious, right? I expected to hear Jacinda was experiencing a nasty complication, or that her body hadn't fully adjusted to new medicine she'd been receiving.

My pulse quickened when I walked into the consultation room. A chaplain sat next to the doctors.

"What is he doing here?" I blurted out.

"He's just here for support."

"Why do I need support?"

Dr. Jewett motioned for me to sit across from her and the others.

"Why do I need support?" I asked again.

Dr. Jewett spoke compassionately. "Jacinda's pineal cyst hasn't changed. That's the good news. But during some of our tests we found something else."

"What do you mean 'something else'?"

"We found a tumor, a significantly large one, on your daughter's brain stem."

"You mean ... cancer?"

"Yes."

How could this be?

Dr. Yang, a physician on Dr. Jewett's medical team, held up an illustrated photograph. "The brain slice of an MRI should look like this—a perfectly symmetrical butterfly. But when we scanned your daughter's brain, we saw a mass."

"Can I see it?"

Dr. Yang nodded, then lifted a horrifying X-ray sheet. Jacinda's "symmetrical butterfly" was distorted and small, like it had been singed over hot coals.

She's only fourteen.

I stared at the coffee cup on Dr. Jewett's desk. The doctors gave me specifics about the tumor but none of it mattered. All I could think about was this: when a person gets brain cancer at fourteen years old, they die. Brain cancer isn't a condition—I knew that—it's a death sentence. And the victim's own body is guilty of the crime.

I left the consultation room in a blurred trance, half in disbelief that I was even in North Carolina, and half convinced the MRI was a mistake. Maybe that ugly mass was the radiologist's thumb. Maybe it was for the wrong patient, and it was somebody else who needed to be told her daughter would never get better. Somebody else who would have to live with that knowledge.

But Dr. Jewett brought me back to reality outside in the hallway.

"We have no time to waste in terms of treatment," she said. "Someone needs to tell Jacinda right now."

She asked me if I wanted to do it, but I declined. Jacinda was too smart. She would see right through me and guess it first. So I asked that Dr. Jewett do it instead.

"And don't sugarcoat it," I told her. "Tell it to her straight, or she'll never trust you again. Just tell her like it is." That's what she always wanted: the pure truth.

We walked into Jacinda's room together. Dr. Jewett pulled up a chair while I sat on the bed and put Jacie's hand into mine.

She was so brave when Dr. Jewett gave her the news—brave enough for herself, brave enough for the doctor, and brave enough for me.

"Am I going to die from this?" she asked.

Dr. Jewett nodded. "Yes, dear, you will."

What a terrible moment for a fourteen-year-old girl. Jacinda wanted to see the world; she wanted to start her own business one day. She dreamed of marrying a farmer or a rancher, someone who shared her love of horses and the outdoors, someone who could give her a dozen children. She wanted to live a long life.

And yet with just four words—"Yes, dear, you will"—it all crashed down, all those hopes and dreams.

Jacinda closed her clear blue eyes and held them shut against the world. When she finally looked up again, her eyes were like glass, her broken dreams projected on the surface—an ethereal movie she would watch for the rest of her days.

Then she blinked, rolled her head to the right, and looked me square in the face.

"Mom, I just want you to know that this is going to be okay."

I smoothed strands of brown hair from her face. "But do you understand? Do you understand what Dr. Jewett is telling you?"

She blinked again, and for a moment I caught my own eyes mirrored in hers.

"Mom, I don't know what this is," she said calmly, "and I don't know why it would happen to a little girl, or why it would happen to me." Then her mouth flipped into the sweetest little smile. "But if this thing that is happening will help one person, any person, anywhere else in the world, find Jesus, even if it is through my death ... then I think it will be worth it."

I couldn't speak. No fourteen-year-old should be required to carry such a weight, and yet here she was, carrying it like a regal queen. Dr. Jewett excused herself, and I crawled into bed to hold my daughter tight against my chest, tight against the world, our two forms draped in sterile sheets.

Jacinda spent the next nineteen days at Brenner Children's Hospital, her health slowly fading. She still couldn't manage food or water. Her doctors put in a nasal feeding tube so she wouldn't starve, but otherwise they were perplexed. Her symptoms just didn't seem to add up. A brain stem *glioma*—the medical name for her tumor—disrupts life, but it couldn't account for what Jacinda was dealing with.

"We're looking for something else—a zebra in a pack of horses," Dr. Jewett explained to me. "Something rare."

It was terrible waiting for someone to tell me *what else* was wrong with my daughter. Only a few months ago I'd been living free and healthy on my Kentucky farm, chasing horses and making fudge; now I was choking antiseptic air in a hospital. Once, I'd awoken to a rooster call. Now I woke to the beep of my daughter's IV.

My only coping strategy was to write in a journal—just as I had on the beach as Tuesday so many years before. Only this time, instead of poetry, I wrote raw and unfiltered thoughts, stained in sorrow, which expressed the heartbreaking reality of my daughter's new fate.

Chapter 17

A CHOICE OF ANOTHER KIND

Jacinda's doctors at Brenner eventually found their "zebra in a pack of horses." She had eosinophilic gastroenteropathy (EG), an incurable disease so rare that Brenner had never before seen a case of it. Only Jacinda's GI doctor had even heard of it.

I was able to take Jacinda home from the hospital, but her new diagnosis started our family down a road of frequent hospitalizations, dire consequences, and complicated medical jargon that would last for years. We saw doctors in Cincinnati, we returned to Brenner, we returned home, we returned to Brenner—a seemingly endless cycle of crash and recovery as the medical bills mounted and our spirits dimmed.

My faith kept me sane—it kept my whole family sane. We had to believe that we were in God's hands. It was the only way for us to face the dark days. And there were many, many dark days.

Eventually we learned Jacinda was actually suffering from not just one form of eosinophilic gastroenteropathy, but five: eosinophilic esophagitis, colitis, gastritis, enteritis, and peripheral blood eosinophilic disease. It was the *combination* of so many ailments that caused her so many problems and kept her so often in and out of the ER.

We also knew that there was only one place she could get adequate long-term treatment for such a devastating and complicated diagnosis: Cincinnati Children's Hospital and its world-class comprehensive clinic, the Cincinnati Center for Eosinophilic Disorders. But there was a catch. The only way for her to receive treatment in Cincinnati was for our Medicaid to cover her in Ohio, which meant we had to become Ohio residents.

Jacinda was in bad shape when I realized I had no choice—that we would have to move to Ohio to save her life. She couldn't keep any food down and was shedding weight at an alarming pace. At first, we tried to take an air ambulance transfer to Cincinnati, but it fell through at the last minute. Then we tried a state-to-state ambulance transfer, but that too didn't come together in time. The only option left was for me to drive us north.

We raced toward Ohio all night on a wing and a prayer, driving seven hours straight through, and when we arrived at the hospital I took Jacinda directly into the ER. Then I hurried to the financial department with a small mountain of forms under my arm. All morning the doctors and I worked in tandem, two figurative hands straining to save one life, and by noon I just managed to turn in the application forms as the nurses wheeled a stable Jacinda into her room. For the moment, she was safe.

I wanted to be with her, to sit by her side until she awoke from anesthesia, but I had other responsibilities that tore me away. Part of our residency required us to find housing, so I sat down in front of a hospital computer and scoured the southern Ohio classifieds, looking for a place to live—just as I had years before on a Florida motel room floor.

I lucked out when I discovered Bethel, a small town about forty-five minutes east of Cincinnati. A landlord had some available apartments for rent, and because I needed housing immediately, I asked him if I could drive out right away. He agreed, and less than an hour later I was standing in front of an affordable apartment, handing him a deposit.

"When do you think you can move in?" he asked.

"Right now."

"Oh, okay," he said. "Well, the place is ready. So your things will arrive later today?"

"Our things are in the back of the truck."

He glanced at my cramped vehicle.

"All of it?"

"All we've got right now." A few friends were driving the rest of our belongings north the following week—we'd left Winston-Salem so quickly I'd only packed a few dresses and Jacinda's medical equipment.

Shannon, Tyler, and I went inside the house and placed our meager possessions on the empty living room carpet. From that moment on, we surrendered our lives to the Children's Hospital. We knew it was Jacinda's last chance at finding a way through her disease.

I brought Jacinda "home" the following afternoon, and we quickly settled into a weekly schedule. Every Monday, Wednesday, and Friday, Jacinda and I made the forty-five minute drive into Cincinnati, where she would see a small army of doctors. On the other days, a home nurse cared for Jacinda while I watched after Shannon and Tyler. We didn't dare leave Jacinda alone for any stretch of time.

I worried about her every day, and I began to worry about Shannon and Tyler too. They hadn't had much in the way of stability or community for a long time. It was always rushing here or rushing there. Now we were finally going to be in one place for a while. I wanted to find a way for them to feel some consistency. And I wanted to get them back in a learning environment.

I didn't expect to find any Amish or Mennonite parochial schools in Bethel—that would be too much to ask for—but I did find a good K–12 public school, Felicity, with a bus stop at the end of our lane. Felicity's principal understood our dilemma, and when I called him he promised they could accommodate any special requests we had on account of our religious beliefs.

It seemed like the best deal we were going to get, but still—I prayed long and hard over whether to send my children to public school. Sure, Felicity was a fine place for learning, but my children weren't accustomed to certain elements of contemporary culture. Shannon hadn't attended public school since kindergarten. Tyler had never been inside of one. Neither knew what to expect. Nor did I.

I was anxious as all get-out the first morning I dropped Shannon and Tyler off in front of that yawning school overhang. I told myself it would be a worthwhile experience if they could just get through the day without being bullied mercilessly. Therefore I was totally surprised, hours later, when they arrived home from the bus stop all smiles. They loved it!

Tyler couldn't wait to tell me about his teacher Miss Goodpastor, a world traveler, and Shannon feverishly counted how many friends she'd made. They were excited to go back the next day, and in the weeks to come, both of them thrived in their new environment.

Shannon's athleticism so impressed her PE teacher that she was placed on the girls' varsity softball team as a freshman, and after I bought some culottes for her to wear in lieu of the uniformed shorts, she laced up her glove as the school's starting second baseman. And Tyler, who loved a good challenge, auditioned for the lead role in *Wild Pecos Bill*—and won the part! My friend Tina drove up from North Carolina and sewed his costume: a vest and corduroy chaps. He played a wonderful Pecos Bill; I'd like to think he drew on our rustic Kentucky experience for his character's "motivation."

And yet, as the school year went on, my children still faced challenges on account of our Plain background.

Shannon began to struggle once she learned her new friends

were smoking cigarettes, stealing beer from their parents, and experimenting with boys. She saw clearly that some of her friends exhibited this behavior out of poor self-esteem or unhappiness—a few even told her as much—and she hurt for them. She wished her friends could feel the wholesome, refreshing joy she carried around in her own heart, but it wasn't in her power to give them that joy. She could only tell them where she got it—Jesus—and hope they listened.

It was hard for me to watch Shannon navigate such uncertain seas. I did take some solace, however, in the belief that maybe, as she began to understand her friends, she would also more fully understand me. I had always been truthful with my children—they knew the mistakes I'd made in my past—but once Shannon began to recognize those same mistakes in her friends, she began to see a young Sherry Harris with fresh eyes. She saw why I'd been so strident in my choices. Why I'd fought so hard to find my place. Why my commitment to God could never be halfway.

My family lived in Bethel for nearly ten months all told. Day after day, Jacinda and I galloped back and forth to the hospital to listen as a cadre of doctors offered less hope than before. She wasn't likely to get better. There wasn't much they could do.

As time wore on, I found myself wondering whether we were doing the right thing. Our family had no community—the very thing we'd been searching for since New Port Richey. There were no Anabaptist, Amish, or Mennonite folk to share in our lives. No back brace to keep us upright.

I never told my children, but I pined for the feeling that used to creep up my spine on Sunday mornings, when hundreds of men and women sent their melodies up into the heavens and God sent His love back down. I missed Pinecraft. I missed Sunnyside. I missed Brother Lester. I often thought about what he'd said to me when we'd left Sarasota all those years before:

"Sherry, I have a burden in my heart for you," he'd said. "You are always running, always traveling to someplace else for some different reason. But deep down, you must know that your home is here, with us. One day I pray you'll listen to your heart. One day I pray you'll quit running. And on that day, I think you will look around and find you are in Sarasota, where you've always belonged."

I knew he was right. I *had* spent a lifetime running. I'd always been physically and emotionally packed and ready to go, ready to start over somewhere new where maybe things would be better. I knew this was not the life God planned for me. I knew He wanted to give me a home — a real home, a place where I belonged.

Still, the idea of moving away from Ohio scared me, because it meant taking Jacinda away from one of the most advanced children's hospitals in the world. I wanted what was best for her. But sometimes, as I watched doctors tether her to yet another confounding network of tubes and machines, I wondered if it was just.

Was it right for her to be poked, prodded, and policed, alone and away from her community, until she tired of life? Didn't she deserve to live on her own terms? It was obvious she wasn't getting any better.

These are questions no parent should ever have to face, and no honest parent who has faced them would say they had an answer. I certainly didn't have any answers. But there was someone who did.

Jacinda and I were driving to the hospital on a bleak and rainy Friday morning when she first spoke up about it. She was in the front seat, her feeding tube apparatus — a backpack containing medical supplies and nutrient formula — stuffed into the leg space behind her.

Suddenly she said, "Mom, what would you think about going home?"

"You mean back to Bethel?" I asked. "We have to meet with the gastroenterologist today."

"No,... I don't mean back to Bethel. I mean back to Sarasota."

I watched drizzled exit signs scoot by in the fog. "Jacie, are you sure?"

"I've prayed about it, Mom. I've prayed about it every day. I've talked to Jesus in an MRI machine and during the pinch of an IV line and when I'm drifting off into anesthesia. He's all I talk to, and He's filled my heart with all the answers I need. He wants me to trust in Him, to love Him, and to be with the people who love me."

She stopped for a moment to collect her breath, then she said, "The people who love me ... those people are in Sarasota, I think. Our life is there waiting for us. We should go home."

"Even if it meant being away from your current doctors?" I said. "Away from the children's hospital?"

"Yes."

"Even if ..." I couldn't finish.

"Mom," she said, "if you can't say what needs to be said, then I will say it."

I shook my head. "I can't."

With great effort, she slid her left hand over the gearshift and found my trembling hand. "You were about to ask if I would like to go home, home to Sarasota, even if it is the last place I will ever live."

I nodded.

She looked up at the raindrops spitting from the sky. "Then my answer is yes."

Chapter 18

FEELING ANKLE

When I told Shannon and Tyler we were moving back to Florida they were ecstatic. They both enjoyed Bethel, but it wasn't *home*. Outside of school they had no community, and anytime I was in Cincinnati with Jacinda they were confined to our house. But in Sarasota, with its legions of friends, babysitters, and chaperones, they would be free. All of us would be free.

Even Jacinda's doctors agreed with our idea to move south. They felt sunshine could do her good and that certain water-based exercises might relieve her pain. She would still need weekly care, and biopsies every six weeks, but we all realized the truth of Jacinda's situation: our primary fight against her disease was effectively over.

I knew we were making the right decision, and I grew even more convinced when I began to feel the strength of God's will at our back. He paved the way when an acquaintance of mine, who lived in Sarasota, called me from out of the blue to ask if I wished to rent her house and take over her job cleaning houses while she was out of town. Her offer solved two problems at once—housing and income—so I gratefully accepted. God's hand was gently pushing us back to where Brother Lester said I should've been all along.

We'd pulled up the stakes many times before, but this time was different. And as we drove out of Bethel, headed toward the highway and points south, none of us could keep from smiling. Not even Jacinda.

I signaled the right blinker and turned onto the I-75 highway ramp. Then I heard the loveliest sound drifting up from the backseat. Shannon was singing.

Amazing Grace.

It really was. And we all joined in.

The house in Sarasota was a rundown and dirty place on Rim Road with holes in the walls and broken locks. I realized immediately that it would not do for Jacinda's needs; luckily my job situation was a godsend. The pay was good, and I quickly found that with a little hard work and a wide smile, my clients—mostly rich doctors—were happy to give me an extra tip. And of course my cleaning skills were impeccable. Anyone who'd fought waves of Kentucky mud, ticks, flies, fleas, bugs, and critters came out of it with some serious chops.

Soon my four clients turned into sixteen, and in no time I had enough money to rent a sweet little house on Fairview Drive, just outside Pinecraft. As soon as we moved we fell into a rhythm we hadn't experienced since Marrowbone. Tyler started school at Sunnyside, and Shannon found work at Yoder's Restaurant. Jacinda and I went to the hospital to see her specialists as often as needed, and we flew back to Cincinnati for tests every other month. Everything seemed normal again.

But normal never stays for long. Not in my life at least.

First, there was a brain MRI and spectroscopy at All Children's Hospital—a fantastic pediatric hospital an hour away in St. Petersburg. Jacinda and I went in for a routine checkup. The results were devastating.

Our pediatrician, Dr. Patricia Blanco, confirmed Jacinda's brain tumor, which had been looming in the background for years, as a focal brain stem glioma that had undergone biochemical change. Tests showed significant cell death. Even worse, Dr. Blanco felt the biochemical changes so abrupt that there wasn't much more medical science could do. She suggested we put my daughter in palliative care.

I wasn't familiar with that word—*palliative*—when I first heard it. But I would soon learn that it was nothing I wanted to hear, for palliative care was one step away from hospice, and hospice meant the end.

We were sent to see a palliative specialist who said Jacinda— still only seventeen years old—had what's called a life-limiting illness and therefore should not expect to see her twenty-first birthday. When Jacinda asked whether she should begin to plan her own funeral, her specialist's response chilled me to the bone.

"That would be appropriate," she said.

It just about broke my heart. By leaving Ohio, perhaps I'd meant to rescue Jacinda from her own fate. Maybe I thought if I could remove her from the constant checkups, I could remove her from the consequences of her illness too. But I couldn't. And now we were back on the clock.

I felt a seed of anger take root in my heart. Doctors had just stamped my daughter with an expiration date. Why would God let that be? Jacinda began to plan her own funeral, and my anger deepened. She chose pallbearers and I seethed. Something broke inside of me, just like when my father died. It wasn't fair. Why was *my* daughter planning her funeral? She was kind. She never hurt others or talked down to them. She was strong and pure and loved Jesus Christ. So why was *her* adult life being erased?

My rage reached its zenith one morning when a young girl, Sarah, entered Sunnyside's fellowship hall with an armload of fabric. She was there to cut a dress for a first date. Well, my own daughter was at home looking at fabric swatches too—for her funeral dress.

In that moment, I'm ashamed to say, I hated Sarah. I hated her for what she could do and how she could live, and I hated her for having joy in a world where others suffered. Each snip of her shears cut a hole in my heart. Each soft fabric caress fueled my internal fire.

I couldn't take it. I left in a fury, lest I say or do something I would regret.

How dare she.

How dare she enjoy her life.

How many days would Sarah have that my daughter would not? A thousand? Ten thousand?

I knew my thinking was spiteful, but I couldn't help myself. I was too angry to pray the anger away. Somehow, despite so many desperate car rides to hospitals, despite the long nights wondering if Jacinda would make it through, it was only when she was given an end date that I fully realized I might lose her.

And I wasn't the only one either, for as I drowned in my own grief, Shannon and Tyler drowned in theirs.

Shannon grew so physically sick she had to be hospitalized. At first, doctors feared she might be gestating an eosinophilic disease, which often targets multiple siblings. But once her biopsies came back negative, we came to realize that it was intense guilt making her ill, guilt she felt over having so much while her sister had so little. Shannon went to youth functions while Jacinda stayed at home. Shannon learned to drive while Jacinda seized up in bed. It was too much for her. It was the shame of privilege.

As for Tyler, he missed Jacinda as a model and a playmate. He remembered their frog-catching, calf-chasing days in Kentucky; now he felt she wasn't there for him in that way. It was childish logic forged out of self-preservation, but it was terrible for a mother to watch nonetheless. A light went out between them. He shut down to her completely.

Months passed in this way, with no change in Jacinda but a marked change in the rest of us. We had no way of knowing the time line of loss—when hospice would start, how long she really had—we only knew things were getting worse. Each time she went under anesthesia I feared she wouldn't wake up. Each time a doctor took her behind a closed door I kissed her forehead, saying goodbye for what might be the last time. I checked on her like a mother does a newborn. At night I'd sneak into her bedroom, lift up the sheet near the foot of her bed, and feel her ankle as she slept.

If it was warm, then I knew she was still alive.

One morning around six o'clock, I was lying next to her in bed when she suddenly began to cry.

"Pray for me, Mom," she sobbed. "It just hurts so bad."

"What hurts, Jacie?"

Silence.

"Jacinda?"

I rolled over.

Nothing. Her chest wasn't moving, so I put my hand on her neck. No pulse. No beat. No sign.

I hopped up, hurrying through the house to wake Shannon and Tyler.

"Shannon, where is the phone?"

I tore pillow cushions from the sofa and upended chairs, looking for my cell phone as Shannon tried desperately to wake her sister. Tyler stood vacant and scared near the kitchen sink.

"Shannon, the phone!"

"Mom?"

"The phone, Shannon! Where is the phone!!"

"Mom!"

I ran into Jacinda's room frazzled and out of breath. "It's in here?"

"No," Shannon said, looking up from the bed. "She's breathing again."

"Breathing?"

"Breathing. Here, look." Shannon licked her palm and held it in front of Jacinda's open mouth. "I can feel it."

I felt for Jacinda's pulse. It was weak but definitely there. A bit of color had already returned to her face.

"Shannon, please find the phone for me so I can call an ambulance, okay?"

Minutes later, EMTs were taking Jacinda to Sarasota Memorial Hospital. She was then transferred to All Children's Hospital, where for the next twelve days she fell in and out of consciousness. When she finally came to, she had no memory of what had transpired and only later realized the extent of it when she read her discharge papers. She'd suffered an ALTE: an "Apparent Life Threatening Event." Her neurosurgeon told us the ALTE had been a shutdown response to all the pain. Usually patients don't survive such an event, but Jacinda had. She had gone away and then returned. Where to? Only God knows that.

After the ALTE, a terrible scare, God must've worked hard on all our hearts, because the mood in our house finally lifted. My anger, Shannon's guilt, Tyler's emotional withdrawal — it fell away like autumn leaves. And we watched Jacinda's own faith grow even stronger. Even after such a traumatic event, even as she was subsequently diagnosed with epilepsy, Jacinda woke up each day with love and prayer in her heart. Her strength reminded the rest of us that even her disease was a part of God's Plan, and that what will be, will be.

It may seem strange that my family and I, a rather devoted bunch, struggled so mightily with the idea that "it's all in God's hands." But sometimes the pain is so deep we forget; we let God's Word become an abstraction — a holy wishing well for our desperate needs. We ask Him for miracles, and forget that the miracle already occurred, thousands of years ago, when Christ died for our sins.

Jacinda's faith reaffirmed my own, along with Shannon's and Tyler's. We only needed a nudge, and once we got it, we remembered to simply look into our hearts, and to Jesus, for our answers. It's all that's ever really asked of us.

And often, when we comply, we find God willing and able to answer our prayers.

Six months after Jacinda's ALTE, we went to see her neurologist for a routine exam and found that her medical team had changed its tune.

"You know, Jacinda, I previously classified you as a two-month patient," said our neurologist.

"What is a two-month patient?" she asked.

"It means that back then I believed you had two months to live. And now here we are, months later, and you're still alive. I don't know how to explain it—no one does. Do you know why that is an important thing for me to mention?"

She shook her head no.

"It's important because it means that not me, nor anyone in this hospital, nor anyone in this world, knows how much time you have left."

He paused, allowing her to absorb his words. Then he said, "So what are your plans?"

"For my funeral? It's ready."

"Well, that's fine—I probably would've done the same if somebody had told me what we've been telling you. But I think you should change your thinking. I think instead of planning for your end, you should start with something else."

"What's that?"

"Hope. Do the things you like to do. Spend time with the people you enjoy. Make new friends. Go places. Read. Listen to music. Do what you dream about."

Jacinda smiled brightly, and then, starting that very afternoon, she began taking her doctor's advice. She spent more time with her online friends. She wrote stories about her own life. She read books and built an impressive musical collection.

She has been rewarded for doing so ever since. That day was five years ago, after all. And I haven't snuck in late at night to feel her ankles since.

Chapter 19

MY PLACE

Tragedy has frequently given me great insight into the choices I've made in my life.

When my father passed away, I was forced to reckon with my present. I didn't know who I was without the driving need for his acceptance.

And then, when April died, I was forced to reckon with my past.

It could've been me in that urn.

Finally, there was a tragedy that forced me to reckon with my future, though I'd never wish for such insight at so high a cost.

It concerned a family I loved dearly, a family who'd helped me weather many storms in Kentucky.

The Esh family.

I was sitting in my van outside Tyler's school in early 2010 when I first heard the news. Something seemed wrong the second he emerged from the building with his head down. He walked slowly to my driver-side window and leaned in, his eyes glassy and raw.

"Tyler, are you okay?"

"No."

"What's the matter?"

He rubbed his nose. "Mom, it's pretty bad."

"What's pretty bad?"

"Well, . . . some of your friends died today." I wasn't expecting that.

"Tyler, what are you saying?"

"I don't know—it was an accident. With a semi."

I squeezed the steering wheel. My voice caught.

"Who?"

"Mom, I ..."

I covered my mouth. "Tyler, who?"

"John and Sadie Esh."

"What?"

"John and Sadie," he said again. "They're gone. And Rachel too."

A lump in my throat. I shook my head. *No.*

"Tyler, there must be some mistake."

"There's not."

"R-Rachel's boyfriend, Joel ...," I stammered, "he must be ..."

"Mom, he died too."

This was too much. I flung open the door and fell to my knees. *They can't be gone.* What will Rose do without her parents? I had received a letter from her only a week before; she was a precious friend.

But later, I would find out that Rose had died as well, and that Anna Lynne Esh had died. And Leroy Esh. And Naomi. And her baby.

One semi. Nine lives lost.

I was too weak to stand on my own, much less drive, but I knew where I had to go. Eleanor Miller, one of Shannon's friends, happened to be in the parking lot and came running when I fell to the ground.

She had a driver's license.

I looked up at her from the blacktop.

"Take me to Yoder's Restaurant," I managed to say. "I have to tell Shannon."

In a fog I stumbled to the van, and Eleanor drove us to

Yoder's. She asked the manager to send Shannon outside. Then I took a sorrowful breath and told my daughter that Rachel Esh, with whom she'd swum in the cow pond, with whom she'd shared secret wishes, was gone forever.

I wish I could forget the look of despair on Shannon's face at that moment. I barely managed to catch her in my arms when her legs buckled, and we huddled there, in the parking lot, weeping silent tears.

Word of what happened traveled fast, as did the details of the tragedy.

It seems the Esh family was traveling to an out-of-state wedding when Kenneth Layman, who was talking to his young wife on his cell phone, and who had driven far too many hours without sleep than any commercial truck driver should, suddenly swerved from the southbound lane on I-65. His massive semi barreled through the median and hit the Eshes' van straight on, splitting their vehicle like an egg and dismembering everyone inside but Naomi's two young boys. Kenneth Layman died instantly, leaving his wife with a dial tone on the other end of their call.

The semi caught fire and burned to ash. Arriving policemen found the crash site so gruesome they called off news helicopters and barred media access to the scene. Investigators hauled what was left of the van to an abandoned warehouse, where technicians pried open shaved metal to remove the bodies, and where, hours later, the Marrowbone elders arrived to identify the remains of their dear friends.

People from all over the country made arrangements to attend the funeral. In Sarasota, friends at Sunnyside Church rented a motor home and invited Tyler and me to come along. Shannon, just returned from a vacation, couldn't get off work. And Jacinda was too sick travel.

In all, five thousand people traveled to Marrowbone to lay

the Esh family to rest—quite possibly the largest mass move-
ment of Plain people in American history. Coroners from five
surrounding counties worked in shifts for three days to prepare
so many bodies, eight caskets in all. They lined them up in a long
row and placed framed 8-by-10-inch pictures atop each one.

For me, seeing the face of John Esh was the worst. I could
just tell that he *knew*—at the moment of the crash, he *had understood* what was happening to him, to all of them.

It gave me the same thought I'd had when I first saw my
father's body lying on a gurney: "A man lives for so long, and
this is what is left?"

It seemed so arbitrary, so vacant.

But as the funeral began, as John Henry Smucker sent his
booming voice over the enormous crowd in eulogy for his dear
friends, I saw that there was nothing vacant about this death at
all. It was clear the Eshes, who so loved my family, who brought
nothing but light into my world, would leave nothing but devot-
edness in their wake.

We took turns shoveling fresh dirt over the graves, an Amish
tradition, and when it was my turn, I tossed my shovelful upon
John and Sadie, who were buried together. Then I found the
arms of my friend Sarah Gingerich.

As it happened, a photographer snapped a picture of our
shared sorrow, and that picture flashed through the news cycle
for weeks and weeks—across the world—as newspapers, maga-
zines, and television stations told the tragic story of the simple
Amish community at the crest of the Cumberland River.

Even today, that photograph—Sarah pulling me close to her
chest, my face buried in her shoulder—represents so much more
to me than our grief. It symbolizes how the Plain community
holds all of us close.

It is my back brace, just like Monica said I would find.

We are a strong people. Our strength comes from the way

we care for one another and in the way we continue, even in tragedy, to have faith in God and the hope He provides. Hope for a good life on earth. Hope for life after death. Hope that in our darkest days we are still loved.

My past tells the story of a troubled girl.

My future is the ongoing story of an Amish-Mennonite woman, of a Christian, of a mother, and of a friend.

My place is here, in Pinecraft, with my people.

God wills it. I know this because I feel it in my heart. And since I made my choice for Him, my heart has never led me astray.

HOLIDAY IN PINECRAFT

My name is Sherry Gore, and I am an Amish-Mennonite woman. Though, as you now know, I haven't always been this way.

I've been unwanted—called worthless, a flunkie, trash, by those who were supposed to love me. I've been reckless—living wild through my Tuesday alter ego, street-smart but naive. I've been ambitious—an LA deejay working hard to rise to the top. And I've been a survivor—both as a new wife under the same roof as a dangerous man, and as a Kentucky wilderness pioneer.

I suppose you could say I've lived a lot of lives. Looking back over them, I see a lonely girl with poor self-esteem, who could never seem to find her place.

But I made it through.

Even when things looked the bleakest, I always *kept going*. And I survived just long enough to realize Jesus Christ could fix what parts of me I'd broken along the way.

For only in His love, and His wisdom, can we be freed from our self-made prisons.

I know this is true because I escaped my prison. I did it by making a choice, one that had always been right in front of me.

So please believe me when I say, to any of you who are struggling, that the way out is ahead of you. *Survive.* Find Him. Don't let the world tell you what you are, or what you can be. Let Him.

Because His words are clear: *With Me, you can be anything.*

The table is set with plain white ceramic dishes and light blue cloth napkins; turkey and stuffing, fresh corn, peas, and mashed potatoes with gravy make for a majestic spread.

It's Thanksgiving in Pinecraft, and as I look around my oak dinner table, I see everyone that I love: Tyler sits next to his girlfriend, Mary, her hand in his. She's found her place with him, and with me, after her own life of trouble. We have that in common. I hope she sees in me a mother and a friend; I certainly see in her the type of second chance my sister April never received.

Jacinda lies still on the sofa. Her eyes look sad because they reflect the state of her body, but inside her eyes, behind them and inside her soul, she's lit with the fire of a trillion suns. She knows she is loved — by her family, by her friends, and by God above.

Shannon calls while I serve the potatoes. Her first child is due in January, and soon I'll fly up to Canada for the birth. When her husband, Richard, joins her on the phone, their voices resound in perfect harmony. And soon, that choir of love will be joined by a third.

Then there is Toby, who visits on occasion, and who has joined us for Thanksgiving. He looks older now, an aging rocker, and he clipped his brilliant blond locks years ago. He's often more thrilled about my career than I am. He will always be a part of our family, even though we no longer live under the same roof.

After we say grace, I move from one setting to the next, serving food to the people I care for so deeply. My life hasn't been an easy one, but whose life is?

I quit starting over and I found my place.

I made a choice fifteen years ago and I stuck to it.

Amen.

Jacinda Michelle Gore
March 18, 1990 — February 6, 2015

"Be thou faithful unto death, and I will give thee a crown of life." Rev. 2:10
(One of Jacinda's favorite verses)

On February 6, 2015,

Jacinda Michelle passed away

due to complications from her various ailments.

She died surrounded by family and friends.

Even in her final moments,

her faith, her strength,

and her kindness remained irrepressible.

She will be missed.

ACKNOWLEDGMENTS

I would like to thank my editors Carolyn McCready and Bob Hudson at Zondervan for their immense work in helping me distill an entire life into an authentic and engaging reading experience. I would also like to thank my colleague and friend Tamela Hancock Murray for encouraging me to write this book and for always standing tall at my side. My friend Ann Mast also deserves my thanks. She is known as "the mom" at my house for sharing her nurturing heart; her support contributed hugely to my efforts to complete this book during a difficult time.

Lastly, a special thank you to author Nancy E. Turner; your book *These Is My Words* inspired me to pour light upon sometimes–dark corners of my life in order to fully understand what I truly believe, and why.